KU-251-850

915.2

**Books are to be returned on or before
the last date below**

COUNTRY STUDIES

JAPAN

Michael Witherick

Series Editor: John Hopkin

Heinemann Library
Halley Court, Jordan Hill, Oxford OX2 8EJ
a division of Reed Educational & Professional Publishing Ltd
Heinemann is a registered trademark of Reed Educational & Professional Publishing Ltd.

OXFORD MELBOURNE AUCKLAND
IBADAN JOHANNESBURG GABORONE
BLANTYRE PORTSMOUTH NH (USA) CHICAGO

First published 1998

00 99 98
10 9 8 7 6 5 4 3 2 1

British Library Cataloguing in Publication Data

Witherick, M.E. (Michael Edward), 1936 –
    Japan. – (Country studies)
    1. Japan – Social conditions – 1945 – – Juvenile literature
    2. Japan – History – 1952 – – Juvenile literature
    3. Japan – Description and travel – Juvenile literature
    I. Title
    952'.049

ISBN 0 431 01402 7 (Hardback)
    0 431 01403 5 (Paperback)

Typeset and illustrated by Hardlines, Charlbury, Oxford OX7 3PS
Printed in Hong Kong by Wing King Tong Co. Ltd.

Acknowledgements
The publishers would like to thank the following for permission to reproduce copyright material.

Maps and extracts
p.11 C Japan Map Centre, Tokyo, Japan; **p.20 B** extract from 'Promises and tears mingle with Japan's settling dust' by Kevin Rafferty in *The Guardian*, 21 January 1995.

Photos
p.4 A Science Photo Library; **p.6 A** Michael Witherick; **p.7 C** Michael Witherick; **p.9 C** Panos Pictures; **p.13 C** PA News; **p.15 B** Nigel Hicks; **p.15 C** Panos Pictures; **p.17 B** Environmental Images; **p.18 A** Axiom Photographic Agency; **p.19 B** Spectrum; **p.20A** SYGMA; **p.22 A** (top) Corbis; **p.22 A** (bottom) Tony Stone; **p.24 B** Panos Pictures; **p.25 C** Eye Ubiquitous; **p.31 C** The Kansai Electric Power Company; **p.32 B** Michael Witherick; **p.33 C** Seagaia Ocean Dome complex; **p.34 A** Robert Harding; **p.35 C** Corbis; **p.37 D** Robert Harding; **p.40 A** Science Photo Library; **p.41 D** Geoff Howard; **p.43 C** Spectrum; **p.43 D** Spectrum; **p.46 B** Cephas; **p.47 D** Kansai Airport; **p.48 B** Tony Stone; **p.49D** Japan National Tourist Organization; **p.49 E** Japan National Tourist Organization; **p.53 C** Eye Ubiquitous; **p.54 A** Panasonic; **p.56 A** Robert Harding; **p.56 B** Panos Pictures; **p.57 C** Still Pictures.

Cover: background, Panos Pictures/Jim Holmes.
foreground, Robert Harding Picture Library.

The publishers have made every effort to trace the copyright holders. However if any material has been overlooked or incorrectly acknowledged, we would be pleased to correct this at the earliest opportunity.

Contents

1 INTRODUCING JAPAN

A nation of islands

▶ Where is Japan located?
▶ What are its main physical features?

Japan is an island nation located 200km off the east coast of Asia and separated from it by the Japan Sea. Japan is also a nation of islands. There are four main islands and about 3900 others forming an **archipelago** (photo **A**).

The Japanese archipelago stretches over more than 20 degrees of latitude. In the north, the island of Hokkaido reaches almost as far as Sakhalin – part of Russia. In the south the Ryukyu Islands reach almost to Taiwan.

Plate margins and island arcs
Japan is located on a very unstable part of the Earth's surface where three **tectonic plates**

meet (map **C**). Along the **plate boundary** are **fold mountains** and **island arcs**. For example, the Bonin Islands Arc has been formed where the Pacific Plate and Philippine Plate rub against each other. These two plates are dragged under the Eurasian Plate (diagram **D**). This causes the Earth's crust to be pushed up into a series of fold mountains. Mountains form the backbones of the four main islands. Because of the movement of these three plates, volcanoes and earthquakes are an important part of Japan's geography.

A Satellite image of Japan and the Asian coast

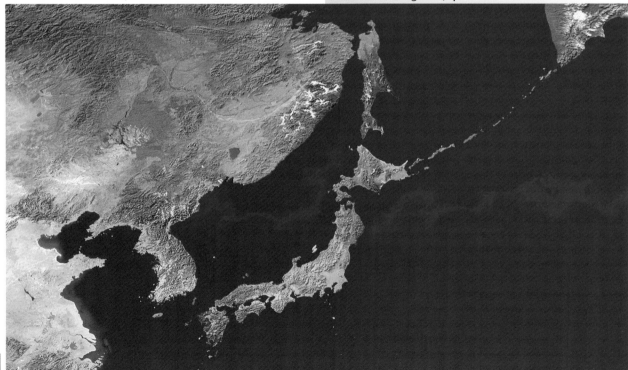

	No. of islands	Share of land area (%)	Share of population (%)	Share of GDP (%)
Hokkaido	263	22.1	4.6	3.8
Honshu	1 546	61.1	80.3	84.4
Shikoku	472	5.0	3.4	2.6
Kyushu	1 641	11.8	11.7	9.2
Total	3 922	377 801km²	125.2 million	$1 022 billion

B Japan's main islands

C Arcs, islands and neighbours

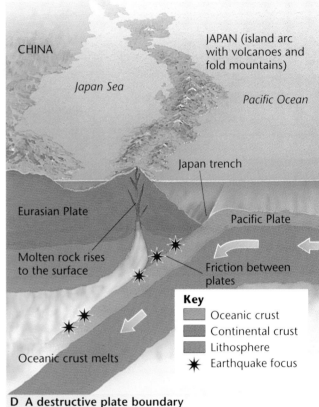

D A destructive plate boundary

FACT FILE

Naming the country

The Japanese refer to their country as *Nippon*. It means 'the place from where the sun rises'. This description was first used in a letter sent to China by a seventh-century Japanese prince. He wanted to describe the location of the lands that he ruled. Even to this day, Japan is known as the land of the rising sun. The national flag (the *Nisshoki*) shows a red sun. Japanese people are called *Nihonjin*. Outsiders and foreigners are called *gaijin*.

The origin of the name 'Japan' is much less certain. One possibility is that it came from the word 'Yatpun', the name used by people in southern China to describe the islands that are now Japan. Early Dutch traders and settlers were the first to call the islands 'Japan'.

A changing nation

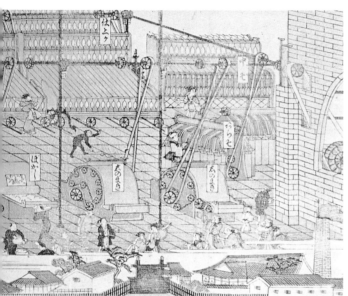

A The modernization of Japan

Isolation and national unity

Some of the answers to Japan's success today can be found in the past. For over 200 years Japan was isolated from the rest of the world. Japan's rulers, the *shoguns*, believed this was the best way to stop Japan becoming a colony of a country in Europe. But by the middle of the nineteenth century it was obvious Japan was falling behind Europe and the USA in technology, weapons and wealth.

Modernization and expansion

In 1867 a revolution brought about important changes.
- The emperor replaced the shogun as leader of all Japan.
- Japan opened up to foreigners, new ideas and technology.
- New industries were set up, especially the making of weapons.
- New roads and railways were built.
- The education system was improved.

These changes were successful but they brought more problems. Industry grew, but it needed more raw materials and energy than the country

had. The population grew, but Japanese farmers could not supply the people with enough food. So Japan began invading its neighbours, starting with Taiwan, Korea, Manchuria and parts of China. This aggression drew Japan into conflict with the USA and its allies, including the UK, during the Second World War and so the war spread to the Pacific (map **B**).

Defeat and reconstruction

The Second World War was a disaster for Japan. In 1945 Japan surrendered after the allies dropped atomic bombs on the industrial city of Hiroshima and the port of Nagasaki. Much of the country was in ruins and the

Key
▨ Extent of empire

0   2000 km

U S S R

Sakhalin (1905)

Kiska

MONGOLIA   Manchuria (1932)

Kurile Islands (1875)

Korea (1910)

JAPAN

C H I N A

Bonin Islands (1861)

Midway Islands

Ryukyu Islands (1876)

Mariana Islands (1918)

Furthest limit of conquest 1941–45

Taiwan (1895)

Caroline Islands

Marshall Islands

N

AUSTRALIA

B The growth of the Japanese empire

C Booming Japan: Kashima in the 1960s

people were badly depressed. Japan had lost **face**. Little changed for five years. But in 1950 **communist** China and North Korea invaded South Korea. The USA realized Japan might be the next country to fall to the communists. It was better to have Japan as an ally rather than an enemy. With American help, Japan was on the road to recovery.

The economic miracle

From 1955 the economy grew fast. Heavy industries like iron and steel, shipbuilding and petro-chemicals prospered (photo C). Consumer industries made a growing range of products, such as electrical goods, cars and cameras. By 1968 Japan had become the world's second most powerful economy – a ranking it has kept ever since. This period of fast growth is often called the 'economic miracle'.

The Oil Crises and low growth

In 1973 and 1979 the price of crude oil rocketed. Unfortunately for Japan, its heavy industries were thirsty for oil. In fact three-quarters of Japan's energy came from oil, so Japan had to rethink its whole economy. Since 1973 the economy has grown much more slowly. But Japan has kept its place as a superpower by making some important changes.
• It uses energy from more sources.
• Energy is used more efficiently.
• Heavy industry has been slimmed down.
• High-tech industries have grown.

Most worrying for Japan in the late 1990s is competition from other industrial countries, especially the 'Asian Tigers' (South Korea, Taiwan, Singapore and Hong Kong). They are beginning to snap at Japan's heels.

FACT FILE

The birth of a nation

In the first century, Japan was a collection of more than 100 small, independent kingdoms scattered over the four main islands. By the fourth century, one of these kingdoms had grown so powerful, it dominated the western half of Honshu, the northern half of Kyushu and all of Shikoku. The family which ruled it became the imperial family. The emperor today, Emperor Akihito, is a direct descendant.

In the eighth century, the power of the emperor began to weaken. Powerful families became feudal lords (*daimyo*) over large areas of land

with many peasants. These daimyo grabbed much of the land and made great fortunes. The families in their turn were overthrown by a warrior class (*samurai*) which the feudal lords had created to keep their peasants under control. The rule of the warrior class through their leaders, the *shoguns*, lasted nearly 700 years, coming to an end in 1867. Early in the seventeenth century, the ruling *shogun* broke off all relations with foreign countries, expelled foreigners and refused to allow foreign travel. In the 150 years of isolation that followed, Japan became a unified nation.

Japan and the Asian Pacific region

▶ Why is the Asian Pacific region so successful?

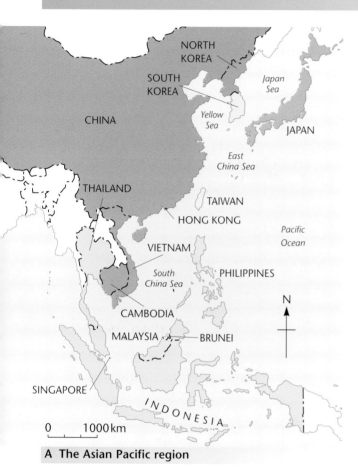

A The Asian Pacific region

Leading a dynamic region

The Asian Pacific region is made up of the fourteen countries of East Asia that face the Pacific Ocean (map A). Japan has been the most economically successful country so far, but other countries are quickly catching up. Today the region produces about a quarter of all the world's economic wealth. It is fast becoming the centre of the global economy. By the year 2000 it is estimated that the region will have half the world's population.

Why is the region doing so well? Partly it is because:
• the countries are keen to enjoy better living standards
• they see Japan as a shining example they can follow

• between them they have raw materials, energy and plenty of low-paid workers
• they can produce goods that are in demand at competitive prices.

The Asian Pacific countries can be divided into four groups (by colour on the map) based on their wealth. The difference between the wealthiest and poorest countries is huge (see table **B** where the colours match the map).

Low-income countries
The low-income countries are all **communist** countries. They have economies which work in a rather different way to the **market** (**capitalist**) **economies** of the other ten countries. Things are beginning to change in all of these countries, especially China. China is an 'awakening giant', with its huge population and rich natural **resources**.

Lower middle-income countries
The lower middle-income countries all have economic growth and rising living standards. Manufacturing industry is behind much of this growth. These countries have plenty of natural resources. Three of them are nations of islands, so building good transport links is a major challenge. Thailand does not have this problem, and farming and tourism are more important here than in the other three.

Higher middle-income countries
In the higher middle-income countries manufacturing industry has been booming for over 25 years. All these countries are small in area and in population. Another name for the four of them is the 'Asian Tigers'. In 1997 Hong Kong was handed back to China. It remains to be seen whether this will continue to be a dynamic area under its new ownership. Brunei is a special member of this group. It is one of the richest countries in the world. It is a big oil producer, with a tiny population and little industry.

Economies	Ranking	GDP per person ($)	GDP ($billion)
High income	1 Japan	36 863	4 509.9
Higher middle income	2 Singapore	24 024	68.9
	3 Hong Kong	21 752	131.8
	4 Brunei	17 611	4.6
	5 Taiwan	11 415	241.2
	6 South Korea	8 616	379.6
Lower middle income	7 Malaysia	3 668	70.6
	8 Thailand	2 131	124.9
	9 Philippines	973	63.9
	10 Indonesia	765	144.7
Low income	11 Vietnam	579	38.3
	12 North Korea	553*	12.7
	13 China	353	413.7
*estimates	14 Cambodia	94	0.9

B Asian Pacific countries – a league table of economic growth and wealth (1992)

C Singapore today – a model state?

High-income countries

At the moment, Japan is the only high-income country in the region, with the highest wealth per person. It also has by far the biggest economy. China is its nearest rival.

The Asian Pacific region will become even more powerful and influential in the twenty-first century. For the time being, Japan will remain the superstar. But all these countries need to remember that economic success also has its costs.

FACT FILE

The Asian Tigers

Hong Kong, Singapore, South Korea and Taiwan are known as the 'Tigers'. They are known as this because of their high rates of economic growth and the speed at which they are catching up with Japan. All are small countries with high population densities. Manufacturing industry has been important in their economic growth. Because of lower labour costs, business has gradually been taken from Japanese firms. For example, South Korea and Taiwan have been doing well in shipbuilding, textiles and electrical goods. Hong Kong and Singapore now compete with Tokyo as major financial centres.

	Average annual growth in GDP (1990–94) (%)	Population density (1992) (per km²)	Employment in secondary sector (1995) (%)	Employment in tertiary sector (1995) (%)	Average income (1995) ($)
Hong Kong	5.2	5481	35	64	17 860
Singapore	8.3	4650	35	65	19 310
South Korea	7.6	444	36	47	7670
Taiwan	6.5	586	39	50	11 000
Japan	2.1	331	34	60	31 450

2 THE PHYSICAL ENVIRONMENT

Land

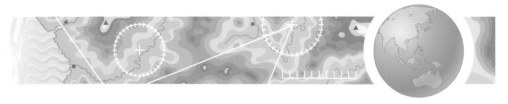

▶ Why is space a scarce resource in Japan?
▶ How has Japan tried to overcome this?

A *shortage of space*

Japan has a big problem – three-quarters of its land area is mountainous and of no use for settlement. Less than a fifth of the country is lowland. Population and economic activity are concentrated here (map **A**). Usable space is a scarce **resource** in Japan.

Lowland Japan

The shortage of space is made worse because Japan's lowland is broken up into many small **plains**. Most of these plains are located along the coast and are cut off from each other by uplands (map **B**). Linking the lowlands together by road and rail has been very expensive, but Japan's transport engineers have become very good at building tunnels and bridges. The island of Shikoku, with the smallest amount of

lowland, poses some of the worst transport difficulties. The biggest lowland is the Kanto Plain, on Honshu. The two largest cities in Japan – Tokyo and Yokohama – are here.

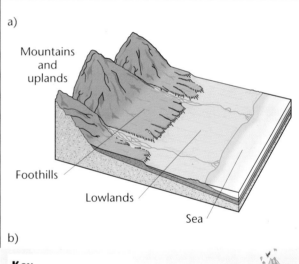

a)

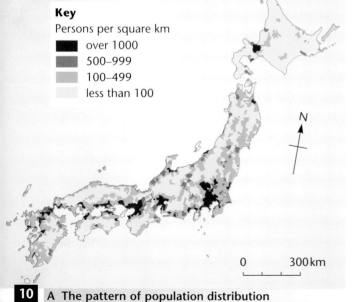

Key
Persons per square km
- over 1000
- 500–999
- 100–499
- less than 100

10 **A The pattern of population distribution**

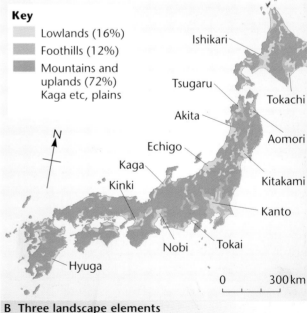

b)

Key
- Lowlands (16%)
- Foothills (12%)
- Mountains and uplands (72%)
  Kaga etc, plains

B Three landscape elements

C Japanese map of Hiroshima

Upland Japan

Mount Fuji (3776m) is Japan's highest mountain. There are fourteen others over 3000m; most of them are old volcanoes. They are part of the Hida Mountain chain that runs the length of Honshu along a boundary between three **tectonic plates**.

The rest of the uplands are not so high but they are cut into by deep, narrow valleys with steep sides and thin soils. So they make transport links difficult and are not much good for farming. The main value of the uplands is their forests. The uplands also offer people opportunities for leisure – peace and quiet, hiking, climbing and winter sports.

Between the lowlands and uplands are the foothills. Although the soils are not very fertile, they are used for farming because land is scarce.

FACT FILE

Highest mountains

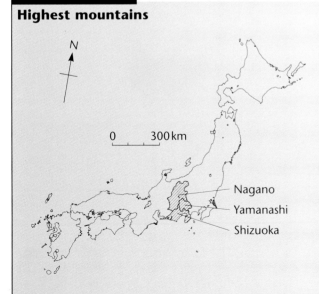

Mountain	Location (prefecture)	Height (m)
Fuji	Shizuoka	3776
Kitadake	Yamanashi	3192
Okuhotake	Nagano	3180
Aino	Shizuoka	3189
Yariga	Nagano	3180
Azuma	Shizuoka	3141

Slope of land (% of land area)					
3° and less	8°	15°	20°		30° and over
14%	15%	24%	16%	23%	8%

Climate

▶ What are the features of Japan's climate?
▶ How does the climate affect people?

Climatic contrasts

Japan's islands stretch over 20 degrees of
latitude so there are big differences in climate
between the north and south (graph **A**). There
are three types of climate.
- Hokkaido has a **continental climate** with
  cool summers.
- Northern Honshu has a continental climate

with warm summers.
- Southern Honshu, Shikoku and Kyushu have
  a **humid subtropical** climate.

A climate of six seasons

Japan's climate varies from season to season, as
well as from place to place. There are six
seasons (diagram **B**). The two rainy seasons,

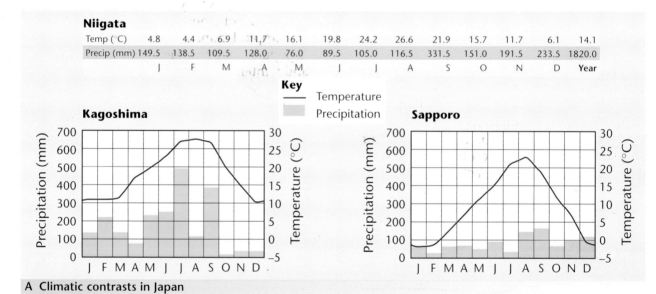

Niigata													
Temp (°C)	4.8	4.4	6.9	11.7	16.1	19.8	24.2	26.6	21.9	15.7	11.7	6.1	14.1
Precip (mm)	149.5	138.5	109.5	128.0	76.0	89.5	105.0	116.5	331.5	151.0	191.5	233.5	1820.0
	J	F	M	A	M	J	J	A	S	O	N	D	Year

Key
— Temperature
▨ Precipitation

A Climatic contrasts in Japan

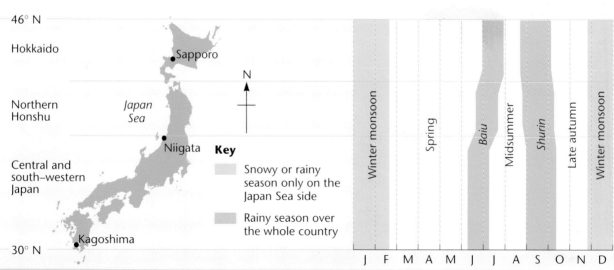

B The six seasons

C Battling against a typhoon

when the **polar front** passes over Japan, are called *baiu* and *shurin*. The length of the hot, humid midsummer ranges from two months in the south to half that in the north. The winter monsoon is a season of bitterly cold north-westerly winds blowing from high pressure in Siberia and bringing rain and snow.

The good news for farming

Temperature and rainfall are important to farming. Rice is the main food in Japan, so levels of heat and moisture must be right for this crop. Rice will grow on the lowlands over most of the country – in fact in the south there can be two crops a year. Because the climate is so varied a range of other crops can be grown across the country.

Tourism

The climate of Japan is a **resource** which is useful for tourism.
- Winter skiing is very popular in the mountains of Honshu and Hokkaido.
- The tropical climate of Kyushu and Okinawa is popular for sunshine breaks in summer and winter.

The downside

The Japanese climate is not all good news. Snow is a problem in winter in the north and on high ground, making transport difficult. Melting snow and the heavy rains of the two wet seasons cause flooding. **Typhoons** track towards Japan between July and November, bringing torrential rain and strong winds (photo C). They are one of Japan's worst hazards.

Water and coasts

Japan's rivers

Japan's rivers drain into either the Pacific Ocean or the Japan Sea. Because nowhere in Japan is very far from the sea, rivers are short. The longest river, the Shinano, is only 367km long (map **A**).

In the mountains, rivers are fast flowing in deep valleys. On the lowlands the rivers become wider and shallow. Many rivers have built high banks called **levees** which raise the river channel above the level of the lowland. This helps farmers, who can drain water off to irrigate their rice fields. But if the river banks break, there is a risk of flooding.

The risk of flooding is worsened after heavy rain, perhaps caused by a typhoon, or when the snow melts suddenly in spring. **Surface runoff** reaches upland rivers quickly because of the steep slopes, so rivers rise quickly. This fast reaction shows in the sharp **hydrograph** of Sendai (map **A**). To reduce the risk of flooding, gates have been built to hold back flood waters. In the lowlands, levees have been raised even higher.

Lakes

Japan's uplands contain many small lakes, often in the craters of old volcanoes. Some are used as reservoirs to supply water to factories and homes. Others are used to generate hydro-electric power (HEP). Many, like the lakes around Mount Fuji, have become tourist honeypots. They offer attractive scenery and opportunities for water sports.

The coast

Since Japan is an **archipelago**, it has a very long coastline. The coastline is made even longer by many small headlands and bays. This coast has created some important opportunities for the Japanese.
- Japan's sheltered bays have provided good locations for ports.
- Coastal shipping has helped link up settlements along the coast.
- Fishing has always been an important source of food and work for the Japanese.

Once the coastal waters were rich in fish, but overfishing has reduced stocks dramatically. Fish now mainly comes from international seas or from fish farms.

A Mean annual hydrographs for two rivers

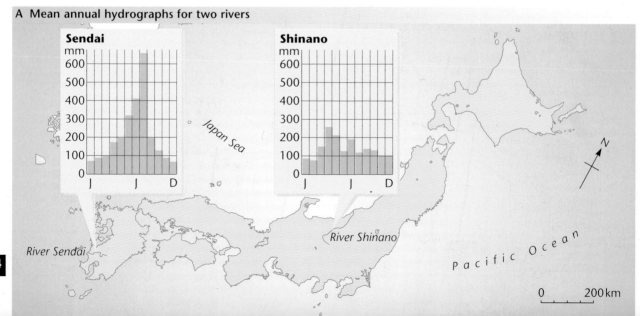

LAKE BIWA

Lake Biwa
By far the biggest lake is Lake Biwa. In the past, it was famous for its beauty. Unfortunately its location close to the cities of Kyoto and Osaka has led to conflict over its use. It is heavily used by people for leisure, but it is also used as a source of water. It has shrunk in size and become polluted by sewage and industrial waste.

B Lake Biwa

THE INLAND SEA

C Farming seaweed

The Inland Sea separates the islands of Shikoku, Honshu and Kyushu. Because its waters provided fish and shelter for shipping, and its shores provided lowland for settlement and farming it was settled early in Japanese history. Since then some of the coastal settlements have become major port cities, such as Hiroshima, Kurashiki and Ehime. The coast provides good anchorages for today's huge supertankers bringing oil and industrial raw materials. Land reclamation created the extra space needed for new large-scale industries. Today, fish-farms in the waters of the Inland Sea produce fish, shellfish and seaweed – all important foods in Japan. But industrial pollution is a problem.

FACT FILE

Rivers and lakes
Major rivers

	Location (prefectures)	River basin area (km²)	Length (km)
Tone	Gumma, Chiba	16 840	322
Ishikari	Hokkaido	14 440	268
Shinano	Nagano, Niigata	11 900	367
Kitakami	Iwate, Miyagi	10 150	249
Kiso	Nagano, Aichi	9100	227
Tokachi	Hokkaido	9010	156

Major lakes

	Location (prefectures)	Surface area (km²)	maximum depth (km)
Biwa	Shiga	670.5	103.8
Kasumigaura	Ibaraki	167.6	7.3
Saroma	Hokkaido	150.4	19.6
Inawashiro	Fukushima	103.3	93.5
Nakaumi	Shimane, Tottori	86.8	17.1
Kussharo	Hokkaido	79.4	15.0

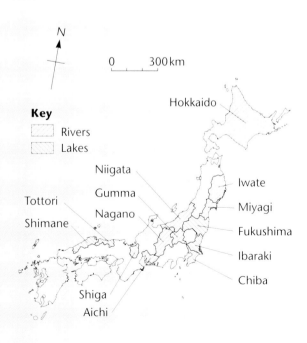

Key
Rivers
Lakes

Natural hazards

A dangerous environment

A **natural hazard** is a natural event that threatens damage and destruction. Japan is quite a dangerous part of the Earth with a range of natural hazards. What matters to people is how often and where hazards occur, how much damage they can cause, and what can be done to avoid this.

Volcanoes and earthquakes

A number of hazards occur because Japan is located on an unstable part of the Earth's crust, where three **tectonic plates** meet. Japan has about ten per cent of the world's active volcanoes (map **A**). Volcanic activity is going on all the time somewhere in Japan but it is not violent. More worrying are the volcanoes that lie **dormant** for hundreds of years and then suddenly come to life. Mount Fuji is a volcano thought to be extinct, but who can be certain?

Earthquakes are frequent in Japan. Many places have as many as 100 in a year. Most of these are weak, but some are very destructive. Earthquakes often set off other hazards, especially landslides and **tsunami**. Tsunami are huge tidal waves caused by earthquake tremors stirring the sea. They cause flooding and death in the coastal lowlands.

Typhoons

Between three and thirty **typhoons** a year strike Japan between July and November. These revolving tropical storms bring very high winds, sometimes up to 200km/hour, causing enormous damage. Torrential rain falls, often 300mm in 24 hours, causing floods and landslides (photo **B**).

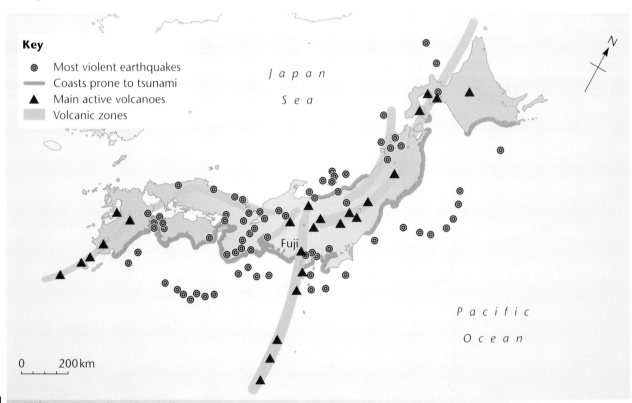

Key
- ◎ Most violent earthquakes
- ▬ Coasts prone to tsunami
- ▲ Main active volcanoes
- ▨ Volcanic zones

Japan Sea

Fuji

Pacific Ocean

N

0   200km

A Volcanoes, earthquakes and tsunami

B Typhoon damage: a landslip following heavy rain

Floods

Floods are also caused by heavy rain in the two wet seasons and by melting winter snow. They are made worse by the steep gradients of the rivers which descend suddenly onto coastal plains and cause a lot of damage because the plains are often heavily populated.

Landslides

Landslides are the most frequent and widespread of all Japan's natural hazards. Once heavy rain soaks into loose soil or rock on steep slopes, this material can easily slip downhill, slowly or with a sudden rush.

Landslides are often set off by earthquakes or by people's activities, such as clearing slopes of vegetation.

Counting the cost

The Japanese live in a very hazardous environment. They can do little to reduce the number or frequency of natural hazards. Their only choice is to try to reduce the risk of death and serious damage as much as possible by being aware of the dangers and making careful use of the land.

Table C gives some idea of the amount of damage caused by natural disasters in a typical year. Except when there is a major earthquake, death and injuries are fairly low.

People –	killed	95
	injured	425
Buildings –	ruined	1 397
	flooded	102 438
Roads –	places destroyed	2 565
Bridges –	swept away	107
Railways –	places damaged	141
Communications broken		107 993
Boats –	sunk	326
	damaged	174
Rice fields – swept away		5 146
People affected		95 907
Total cost of damage		£3.7 billion

C Hazard damage in 1990

FACT FILE

Hazards caused by people

Not all environmental hazards are linked to natural events. Serious hazards can be caused by human activities. Fire, road accidents and war are three examples. Pollution is another, but in this case the physical environment - air and water - are affected. Japan has suffered a great deal of environmental pollution. It was worst during the 1960s when the country was at the peak of its 'economic miracle'. People's health was badly affected.

The table shows that the levels of some air pollutants have been cut. However, nitrogen dioxide is still on the increase. The major cause is the continuing increase in the number of motor vehicles on Japan's roads.

Air pollution	1965	1991
Sulphur dioxide (ppm)	0.057	0.011
Carbon monoxide (ppm)	6.0	2.2
Nitrogen dioxide (ppm)	0.022	0.029
Suspended dust particles (mg per m^3)	0.051	0.040

ppm = parts per million

The environmental balance-sheet

A Lowland congestion: Nagano on Honshu

The physical environment can have a powerful influence on people, both positive and negative. It gives people opportunities, as well as setting limits on what they can do. By looking at the difficulties and opportunities for Japan in this chapter, we can draw up an environmental balance sheet.

Environmental difficulties

The Japanese are faced by four main environmental difficulties.

- Japan's mountains and uplands make transport difficult.
- There is very little space for agriculture and settlement (photo A).
- Japan has a harsh climate in the north and in the mountains, particularly in winter.
- There are many natural hazards.

There are two other important problems. First, Japan has few minerals, such as iron ore, and few energy **resources**, such as oil. So it is all the more remarkable that it has become a leading industrial nation. Second, Japan's soils are not very fertile. Even on the lowlands, the soil needs careful handling and frequent feeding with fertilizers.

Environmental opportunities

However, Japan's physical environment has been encouraging to people in various ways.

- The sheltered bays and inlets of the coast provide good sites for ports.
- The coastal waters once produced plenty of fish.
- The climate is good for growing rice and other crops.

- The climate is good for different types of tourism.
- The spectacular mountain scenery is attractive to tourists – hikers, climbers, winter sports enthusiasts.

Two other resources have been useful. First, Japan's forests have supplied the country with building timber, fuel and paper for centuries. Second, Japan has many hot springs close to volcanoes. Taking a hot spring bath has always been a popular form of recreation, so many small holiday resorts have grown up around hot springs, especially in the mountains of Honshu and Kyushu (photo **B**).

B A hot spring bath

The environmental balance

You might think that Japanese people have to live in an unfriendly environment, with a shortage of space and frequent natural hazards. But there are also some plus points which may balance things out (diagram **C**).

We can be more certain that the physical environment has had a big influence on Japan's development. Japanese people have made the most of the environmental opportunities and made adjustments for the difficulties. But we need also to remember that people often make competing demands on the environment. For example, there is conflict between farming and urban growth on the lowlands, and between forestry and golf courses in the uplands.

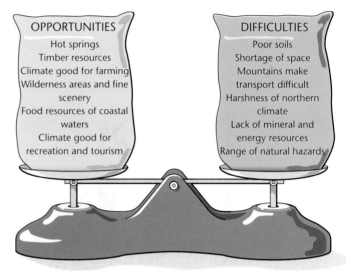

OPPORTUNITIES	DIFFICULTIES
Hot springs	Poor soils
Timber resources	Shortage of space
Climate good for farming	Mountains make
Wilderness areas and fine	transport difficult
scenery	Harshness of northern
Food resources of coastal	climate
waters	Lack of mineral and
Climate good for	energy resources
recreation and tourism	Range of natural hazards

C Japan's environmental balance

FACT FILE

Mineral resources

Japan does have some minerals, but the problem is that there is not enough of each mineral and they are not of a high enough quality. Local coal and iron ore were mined for the iron and steel industry in the nineteenth century. The more accessible and richer deposits have been worked out. Today, it is much cheaper to import supplies. Copper, lead, zinc, chromium silver and gold are still being mined, but in all cases output is declining and imports are increasing. Deposits of uranium are proving useful in supplying fuel for the country's nuclear power stations. The lack of oil and natural gas is probably the most serious shortage.

Since 1955 the number of people employed in mining has fallen from over 400 000 to a mere 25 000. Nearly half of today's Japanese miners are working non-metallic minerals – that is, clays, limestone, sand and gravel.

The Kobe earthquake

▶ **What was the impact of the Kobe earthquake?**

▶ **What lessons were learned?**

A Destruction comes to Kobe

Kobe is the sixth largest city in Japan and one of the world's largest ports. At dawn on 17 January 1995 Kobe was rocked by a series of earthquake tremors. The worst of these reached 7.2 on the Richter scale. In a matter of minutes, Kobe had become a disaster area.

Images of tilted expressways, collapsed buildings, rescuers digging in the rubble for survivors and bewildered people salvaging belongings from ruined homes were soon seen on TV around the world (photo A). It was Japan's worst earthquake for 72 years. The final toll was nearly 6000 people dead, 26 000 injured and 310 000 homeless. 75 000 buildings were damaged or destroyed, with a repair bill estimated at £60 billion.

Two lessons were quickly learned in Kobe.
- The emergency services reacted too slowly and had great difficulty coping with the disaster.
- People suffered deep trauma, many of whom were not physically injured (extract B).

A tearful young woman and her husband returned to their destroyed home. Unsteadily they climbed over the debris to the remains of what had been their first-floor bedroom with the futon still spread on the floor. The woman stooped to retrieve a grimy favourite handbag that she saw peeping out of the dirt, then bowed her head and said a final prayer 'of thanks to God for helping us out alive, of sadness that the family home has been utterly destroyed and for help – to recover and start again.'

She bowed again, stepped back, scrambled down and let a demolition worker swing his bulldozer to flatten what was once home. Her husband put a finger behind his glasses to wipe away a tear. They had not the heart to remove clothes washed overnight in the machine that mockingly seemed to have escaped unscathed.

'It was our family home and had belonged to my husband's father,' the woman explained.
'I don't know where we are going to get the money to build a new one or where we will stay in the meantime, especially if our companies do not start work again. We are five, including two young children and my husband's elderly mother, so it will be hard to cope.'

From 'Promises and tears mingle with Japan's settling dust' by Kevin Rafferty in *The Guardian*, 21 January 1995

B Personal account of earthquake victim

Since Kobe, Japan has begun a thorough review of the whole earthquake issue. Three questions are being asked. They relate to the way people react to a natural hazard (diagram C).

- Is the earthquake hazard being taken seriously enough (**hazard perception**)?
- Is the risk of earthquake damage being under-estimated (**risk assessment**)?
- Is the right sort of action being taken (**risk adjustment**) to reduce the risk of serious damage (**risk reduction**)?

The Kobe earthquake suggests that the answer to all these questions is 'no'. The major problem is the costs of actions such as:

- 'quake-proofing buildings and **public services**
- building sea walls to protect coastal settlements from tsunami
- setting up emergency services
- educating people on what to do when an earthquake strikes.

It is a matter of balancing the costs of these actions against the risk of a strong earthquake occurring. Clearly, there are limits to how much money can be spent on anti-earthquake

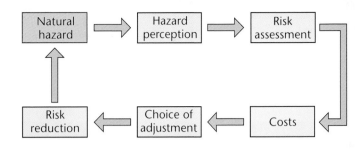

C How people react to a natural hazard

measures. But sometimes there will be earthquakes so strong that they destroy even the most advanced forms of 'quake-proofing.

The basic problem with earthquakes is that we cannot forecast exactly when or where they will occur and with what strength. The Japanese had been expecting a big earthquake to strike one of its major cities. But the architects and engineers believed that by using modern technology they were making new buildings, transport lines and public services reasonably 'quake proof. A few minutes of earth tremors in January 1995 shattered that belief. The clear message from Kobe is that more has to be done to cut the damage threatened by a major earthquake.

FACT FILE

Earthquake name	Date	Magnitude	Deaths	Damaged houses
Great Kanto	01/09/23	7.9	142 807	576 262
Tanazawa Range	15/01/24	7.3	19	1298
North Tango	07/03/27	7.3	2925	16 295
North Isu	26/11/30	7.3	272	2240
Sanriku offshore	03/03/33	8.1	3008	7479
Tottori	10/09/43	7.2	1083	7736
Tonankai	07/12/44	7.9	998	29 189
Mikawa	11/03/45	6.8	1961	12 142
Nankai	13/01/46	8.0	1432	15 640
Fukui	28/06/48	7.1	3895	39 111
Chile earthquake tsunami	23/05/60	8.5	139	2830
Niigata	16/06/64	7.5	26	2250
Tokachi offshore	16/05/68	7.9	52	691
Miyagi offshore	12/06/78	7.4	28	1383
Sea of Japan	26/05/83	7.7	104	1584
SW Hokkaido offshore	12/07/93	7.8	234	3557
Kobe	17/01/95	7.2	6000	75 000

3 THE ECONOMY

Post-war growth

▶ How has Japan become an economic superstar?

The second half of the twentieth century has been a remarkable time for Japan. In 1950 it still lay in ruins after the destruction of the Second World War (photo **A**). The people were in poor health and had lost the will to succeed; defeat had meant a serious loss of **face**.

Today, Japan is the world's second wealthiest nation, after the USA. Its businesses and products are found all over the world. Japanese people are thought of as hard workers, big spenders and lovers of the latest gadgets and fashions.

Explaining the economic miracle

So how has Japan become a world superstar? The answer lies in the growth of the Japanese economy. Three important changes have taken place since 1950:

1   Japan's economy has grown enormously. Although it has slowed down recently, it is still growing faster than rival countries (table **B**).

1945–55	9.1%
1955–65	10.0%
1965–75	8.3%
1975–85	4.2%
1985–95	3.3%

B Average annual rates of economic growth

2   There have been changes in the balance of **primary**, **secondary** and **tertiary** activities which make up the economy (graph **C**).

3   Over the last 25 years, many of Japan's industries and businesses have set up factories and offices in other countries. More and more of Japan's wealth is being created **offshore** – outside the country.

Human resources

Japan has few resources of raw materials or energy. But Japan's **human resources** are very good at producing goods and services. Japanese people have:
- a high standard of education
- a healthy attitude to hard work
- a willingness to try new ideas
- a wish to be part of a team
- a wish for Japan to succeed as a country.

A Changing Japan: Tokyo in 1945 and 1995

Management and organization

The way Japanese businesses are run has also helped the economy, for example by:

- using new technology and production methods
- cooperation between employers and workers
- cooperation between giant companies and many small family firms
- cooperation between the government and business.

MITI

The Ministry of International Trade and Industry could be Japan's 'secret weapon'. For over 40 years it has collected and analysed information from around the world on new products, new technology, new markets and new competition. The results are passed on to Japanese industry and business to help them to decide on new products and services to develop. In the UK and the USA, businesses have to do this sort of research for themselves.

a) % Total employment

	Primary sector	Secondary sector	Tertiary sector
1960	30.2	28.0	41.8
1970	17.4	35.2	47.4
1980	10.4	34.9	54.7
1990	6.0	33.9	60.1

b) % GDP

	Primary sector	Secondary sector	Tertiary sector
1960	12.6	39.0	48.4
1970	5.9	43.1	51.0
1980	3.5	38.6	57.9
1990	2.8	38.4	58.8

C Change in the sectors of the economy

FACT FILE

Government intervention

Although Japan is held up to be a **capitalist** country, the running of the economy has not been left entirely to market forces. In fact, the economy has been carefully managed. The government has frequently stepped in to help and steer the growth of the economy. This intervention includes:

- protecting Japanese agriculture from foreign competition (see cartoon)
- promoting **high-tech industry**
- persuading manufacturing to move to less congested locations outside the Pacific Belt
- managing the value of the Japanese yen, for example in order to stop Japanese goods becoming too expensive for foreign buyers
- controlling **imports**
- keeping the demand for goods and services at a steady level.

Japan is not the only one to protect their agriculture

Farming and the rural economy

▶ How is farming in Japan changing?
▶ What is the impact on rural communities?

A shrinking sector

Only six per cent of Japanese jobs are now in the **primary sector** – farming, fishing, forestry and mining. They create only three per cent of the country's wealth. Farming is the most important of these jobs.

Rice production

Japan now grows over three-quarters of all the rice it needs. New strains of rice, heavy use of fertilizers and mechanization give much higher yields than in the past, and they can now be grown even on Hokkaido with its cold climate. The main rice-growing area is in northern Honshu. However, two harvests a year are possible in the warm south.

Meeting changing demands

Japan's varied climate allows a range of cereals and fruit to be grown. On Hokkaido cattle are kept for meat and milk, and barley is grown for beer and whiskey. In the south of Japan, Kyushu and Okinawa grow subtropical fruits like mandarins and pineapples. All this produce is in greater demand because the Japanese diet and tastes are changing. People are eating less fish, soya and rice. Beer has replaced *sake* as the most popular alcoholic drink.

	1965	1990
Farm households	5 665 000	3 835 000
Full–time farmers	1 219 000	592 000
Part–time farmers	4 446 000	3 243 000
Farms under 0.5 hectares (%)	38	42
Rice (000 tons)	12 409	10 347
Soya beans (000 tons)	230	272
Milk (000 tons)	3 221	8 059
Pigs	3 976 000	11 817 000
Beef cattle	1 886 000	2 703 000
Fertilizers (% production costs)	13	7
Machinery (% production costs)	14	31
Labour (% production costs)	56	37

A Agricultural change (1965–90)

Today Japan produces about 60 per cent of the food it needs, in spite of problems with Japanese farming. Table A gives some information about the dificulties. Government support is needed to keep many farmers in business. Subsidies are given to help meet the costs of fertilizers, machinery and improvement schemes.

FARMING ON THE KANTO PLAIN

Farming on the Kanto Plain

The Kanto Plain is Japan's largest lowland. It has an urban population of over 25 million centred on Tokyo and Yokohama. Large areas of farmland have been swallowed up by urban growth. The farmers who are left can make quite a good living by supplying the cities. Wealthy city people will pay good prices for fresh fruit and vegetables, milk, eggs and flowers. More and more sales are being made at the farm gate.

B Farming for an urban market

PART-TIME FARMING

The Koga family's farm is near Matsuyama on Shikoku. It is an intensive arable farm of only 1.5 hectares. The farm has been in the family for generations – Isao took over the farm when his father died thirteen years ago. Before then he worked as a joiner in Matsuyama and helped with the farm at weekends.

Isao quickly found he was earning less than before and not enough to support the family. He lacked the cash to buy extra land from neighbours. After two years he went back to his old job. His wife and mother now do most of the farm work. Isao and his children help out in their free time.

Two-thirds of the land is used to grow rice and barley (both supported by government subsidies). The other third is used for vegetables, including tomatoes, aubergines and onions. All the produce is sold in Matsuyama or to urban markets in southern Honshu (thanks to the opening of one of the bridge links between Shikoku and Honshu).

Apart from the **inputs** already mentioned, others include fertilizers and herbicides, a rotary digger and a mechanized watering system. The Kogas are also members of a local **cooperative**. This provides bulk–buying and selling facilities as well as advice.

Today, Japan has half-a-million full-time farmers and three million part-timers. Most of these, like Isao Koga earn more from other jobs. Unfortunately, part-time jobs are not enough to keep people in rural areas. Communities are slowly dying as people move to the cities for work. Without government subsidies, many more farms would be abandoned altogether.

C The Koga family's farm

FACT FILE

The Japanese diet
Rice has always been the main food, eaten along with vegetables, fish and 'miso' (a mixture of fermented soya beans, barley and rice). Pickles, some of them very strong, are a popular accompaniment. For centuries, the eating of meat was forbidden because their religion, Buddhism, did not allow it.

Since the end of the Second World War, there have been important changes in what the Japanese eat. Bread has become part of the diet. There has been a great increase in different kinds of meat (particularly beef and chicken) and dairy products. Western-style fast-foods have also caught on, especially with younger people. Most Japanese cities now have their branches of McDonalds, Dunkin' Donuts, Pizza Pan and so on.

Some of the Japanese dishes liked best by foreign visitors are:

- sushi - small balls of specially prepared cold rice topped with slices of raw fish, shellfish, seaweed and a type of omelette. Top sushi chefs are highly sought after.

- tempura - a fritter-like dish of fish, shellfish and vegetables dipped in a light batter and deep-fried in vegetable oil.

- sukiyaki - slices of beef braised together with vegetables in a small amount of liquid seasoned with soy sauce and other ingredients.

Manufacturing

▶ How is industry in Japan changing?

Manufacturing industry has been an important part of Japan's economic miracle. But today, manufacturing creates less than 40 per cent of Japan's wealth and only one-third of jobs.

Industrial changes

Between 1950 and 1973 heavy industries were the most important; for example, iron and steel, shipbuilding and petrochemicals. These industries **imported** large amounts of raw materials and energy. The Oil Crises in 1973 and 1979 made these much more expensive, so product prices went up and Japan's heavy industries became less competitive. Japan had to restructure its industry by building up other types of manufacturing.

Two types of industry have helped to make up for the decline in heavy industry. **Consumer** industries produce a wide range of products from cars to camcorders, pianos to personal stereos for people in Japan and abroad. The other type of manufacturing is **high-tech industry**.

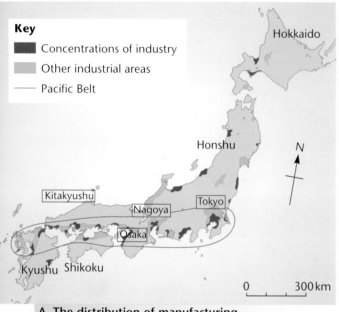

A The distribution of manufacturing

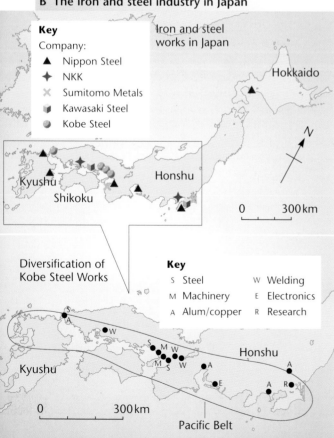

B The iron and steel industry in Japan

KOBE STEEL LTD

Kobe Steel was formed in 1905. Its location in a major port city was useful for importing iron ore and coal. The company expanded in the 1950s and 1960s and set up new smelting works elsewhere in Japan. But in the 1970s foreign competition and falling demand forced the company to make important changes:

- It closed small uneconomic steel works.
- It concentrated steel production in a few large works.
- It diversified by turning factories to other things, such as engineering.

In the 1980s and 1990s the company has **diversified** even more. It has businesses in information technology, robotics and biotechnology. It has also set up around 30 **branch plants** in other countries. These changes have helped Kobe Steel Ltd to survive and prosper in a rapidly changing world.

Distribution

Seventy per cent of Japan's industry is located in the Pacific Belt (map **A**). This helps businesses because they are close to the main markets for their products in the big cities. It is also easier to move products between factories. The main ports for **exporting** products overseas are also here. But there are also costs. Land is more expensive and wages higher, and there is also more traffic congestion and pollution.

YAMAHA MOTOR COMPANY

Honda, Kawasaki, Suzuki and Yamaha produce most of the world's motorbikes. They sell over a million new machines each year in Japan alone. Narrow city roads and traffic congestion make motorbikes a popular form of transport.

The Yamaha Motor Company was set up in 1955 at Hamamatsu, an area with plenty of skilled workers. Today, it produces nearly two million motorbikes a year, most being sold overseas. Two important changes have taken place. First, the company now makes a range of products, including all-terrain vehicles, go-karts, power boats and outboard motors. Second, it has set up **branch plants** (factories) in other countries, especially South-East Asia and South America.

Number of workers in Japan		11 200
Number of factories		10
% share of motorcycle sales in Japan		30
% output –	motorcycles	50
	marine products	21
	power products	11
	car engines	8
	others	10
% total output exported		59
Overseas branch factories –	Asia	6
	South America	4
	Europe	3
	Africa	1

C Yamaha Company statistics

FACT FILE

Craft industries

The Meiji Restoration after the *shoguns* in 1867 marks Japan's beginning as a modern industrial nation. That is not to say that Japan had no industries before that. Far from it, there was a whole range of what are called 'craft industries'. These relied heavily on the manual skills of workers and generally used only small amounts of raw material. Perhaps the most widespread craft industries were:

- silk - a natural fibre made from the silkworm that was then woven into a fabric mainly used in expensive clothing

- ceramics - pottery and porcelain made from local clays and decorated by skilled artists

- lacquer ware - household and decorative objects coated by the thick sap of the lacquer tree. This makes them resistant to damp and corrosion

- swords - originally made as weapons, but later becoming treasured as works of art.

In the middle of the nineteenth century, when Japan began to open its doors to foreigners, there was great interest in some of the products of the craft industries, particularly silk, ceramics and lacquer ware. These were important **exports** for Japan, even up to the beginning of the Second World War.

From high-tech to high street

▶ Why are high-tech industries good for Japan?
▶ What is the tertiary sector and why has it expanded so much?

High-tech industries

An important part of Japan's **high-tech industry** is making machines like computers and satellites that collect and process information. Another is using new methods to make new materials and drugs. These industries are good for Japan because they use small amounts of raw materials and energy. They help keep Japanese industry more efficient and its products ahead of competitors, for example in robotics (table **A**). High-tech industries need a lot of skilled and well educated workers, especially for research and development. So they are important in helping Japan to **restructure** its industry.

Service industries

The tertiary sector is the part of Japan's economy which has grown most since 1950. It has grown as people have become wealthier - as people earn more, they can spend more on services. The **tertiary sector** or **service industries** can be roughly divided into two groups: commercial (profit making) and social (non–profit making) services.

Today about 26 million people in Japan work in profit-making service industries. These include:
• retailing and wholesaling
• transport, communications and information industries
• business and finance
• tourism.

The non–profit making services or social services provide for people's welfare, for example medical care and education, which employ over three million people.

A further ten million people work in the government and other services.

	Japan	USA	Germany	Italy	France	UK
Robots in use 1995	377 025	66 286	51 375	22 963	13 276	8 314
Robots for every 10 000 workers 1994	245	31	51	45	30	17

A World robot production and use, 1994–95

TECHNOPOLIS PROJECTS

There are over 40 new towns being built in Japan which are technopolis projects. Each project has three parts:

• an industrial area of high-tech factories and support services

• a university

• a housing area for workers and their families.

The site chosen for a technopolis should be within 30 minutes' reach of a major city and well connected in terms of national and international transport networks.

The government supports these projects because it is keen to keep Japan a world leader in high-tech industry. It wants each of the prefectures to have a technopolis project. So all parts of the country are involved in the high-tech industry.

MATSUSHITA CORPORATION

Matsushita is one of Japan's major transnational companies with business bases in over 40 countries, especially in SE Asia, N America and Europe, and research and development bases in Japan, Singapore, Taiwan, USA, Germany and the UK. It specializes in electrical and electronic goods:

- home appliances, e.g. microwave ovens, refrigerators
- video and audio, e.g. new wide-screen TVs
- telephone products, e.g. mobile phones, fax machines
- electronics, e.g. semi-conductors, CD–ROM drives.

Matsushita is best known for its Panasonic audio-visual products like the camcorders made at its Osaka factory. They are assembled here from components, many of which are made by small family businesses.

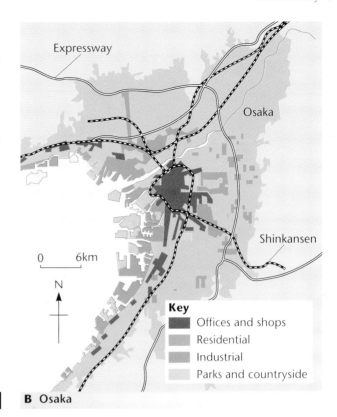

Key
- Offices and shops
- Residential
- Industrial
- Parks and countryside

B Osaka

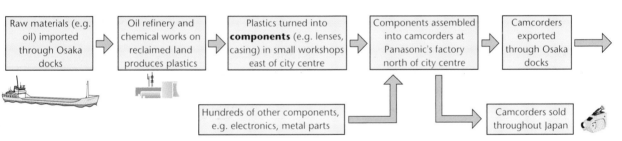

C Systems diagram of Panasonic camcorder production

FACT FILE

Social services

All employers and workers in Japan have to contribute on a regular basis to insurance schemes that will pay for pensions and medical care. They are free to choose between schemes run directly by the government and those run by private companies.

Most other social services are paid for by national and local government through the tax system. These services include help for the unemployed and those on very low incomes, as well as support for families with more than three children.

Most important of all, though, is education. Education is free for the years of compulsory schooling (that is, between the ages of six to fifteen) as long as the children attend a state school. Japanese schools are very disciplined and teachers are highly respected. Exams are taken very seriously and many children from age six up to university entrance, go to private 'crammers' where they receive personal tuition. This takes place outside normal school hours and can be quite costly.

Energy

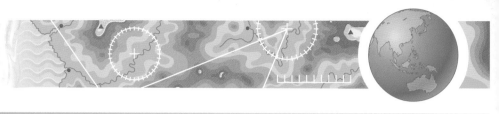

▶ What has Japan done to improve its energy supplies?

Japan's economy has a big weakness – it is short of energy resources. Japan has little oil and has used up its best coal.

The Oil Crises

Until 1973 Japan depended on cheap oil from the Middle East for industry, transport, electricity generation and heating buildings. The Oil Crises in 1973 and 1979 forced Japan to rethink its energy policy.

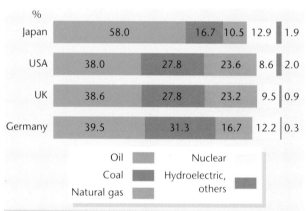

A **International comparison of energy sources (1992)**

%					
Japan	58.0	16.7	10.5	12.9	1.9
USA	38.0	27.8	23.6	8.6	2.0
UK	38.6	27.8	23.2	9.5	0.9
Germany	39.5	31.3	16.7	12.2	0.3

Oil — Coal — Natural gas — Nuclear — Hydroelectric, others

Japan now uses oil more efficiently, and by the year 2000 it will have reduced its dependence on oil from 75 per cent to 50 per cent (graph **A**). But three-quarters of Japan's oil still comes from the Middle East. Japan also uses more energy from other sources. Natural gas provides ten per cent of Japan's energy, imported mainly from Brunei and Indonesia. Almost all of Japan's coal is imported from Australia and China.

Nuclear and hydro-electric power (HEP)

Japan has developed nuclear power to try to reduce oil imports. Japan has one of the biggest nuclear programmes in the world, with 50 power stations operating or being built (map **B**). They provide ten per cent of Japan's energy.

Japan has many mountains and lakes, but most of the rivers and drainage basins are too small to be of much use for HEP. Japan gets less than two per cent of its energy from HEP.

B **The distribution of nuclear power stations**

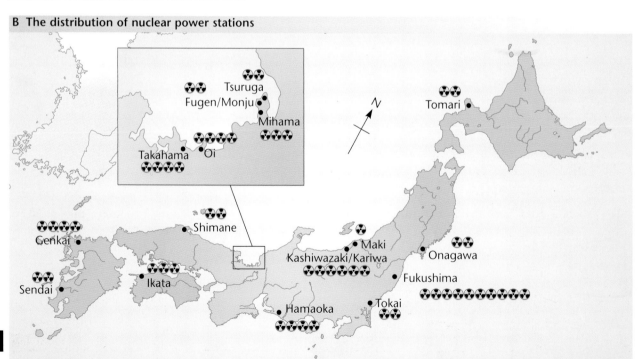

C Nuclear power station at Oi

THE NUCLEAR DEBATE

The nuclear debate
The Oi Nuclear Power Station is one of a group of fifteen that has been built around Wakesa Bay on the Japan Sea coast. This area has been chosen because it is a safe distance away from major centres of population. The sea provides power stations with large amounts of cooling water.

Safety is the main concern in the debate about nuclear power, although in Japan most people are in favour of it (table **D**). There are three main problems:
- the risk of a major disaster, like the accident at Chernobyl in Russia in 1986
- the risk of smaller leaks of harmful radiation
- the problem of what to do with nuclear waste, which needs to be stored safely for thousands of years.

Nuclear power also has some advantages.
- It is a concentrated and powerful form of energy, so it needs less fuel and land.
- It produces small amounts of waste.
- It causes much less air pollution than burning coal, oil or gas.

Alternatives
Today, 84 per cent of Japan's energy comes from overseas. There are worries about nuclear power, so the Japanese are keen to find alternative sources of energy. They are researching wind, **geothermal**, wave and **solar energy**. At the moment, however, none produces enough power at an economic price.

	1984	1994
In favour of more nuclear power stations	64%	67%
Should stop building nuclear power stations	14%	20%
Should stop generating nuclear power altogether	10%	7%
Don't know	12%	6%

D Public opinion about nuclear power

FACT FILE
Energy supply and consumption

	% of Japan's energy supply	
	1970	1995
Oil	72	56
Coal	20	17
Natural gas	1	10
Nuclear energy	0	14
Others	7	3

Energy consumption per person (kg per year)

Japan	3856
Australia	5341
France	4042
Germany	4128
UK	3772
USA	7819

Japan's energy consumption is remarkably low given that it is one of the most successful economies in the world.

Leisure and tourism

▶ What do the Japanese do in their leisure time?
▶ Why is it important to the economy?

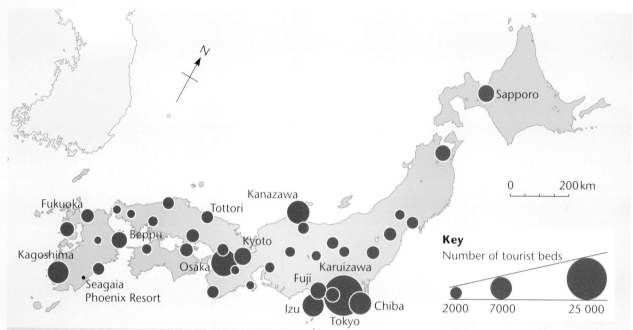

A The major resorts

Japanese people work hard but leisure time is also more and more important. Traditional tourism is still popular, for example spending time at a hot spring resort like Karuizawa (photo **B**) or playing *pachinko* – a type of pin ball. But as people have more time and money to spend, the choice of things to do is widening. Near cities, theme parks, sports centres and golf courses are being built. An example is Tokyo Disneyland, Japan's number one visitor attraction with seventeen million visitors in 1995. Unfortunately, these leisure facilities use up large amounts of farmland. On the coast, marinas are springing up, while ski runs are being carved out of mountainsides.

More leisure time and wealth allows more people to travel abroad, eleven million in 1995. In the opposite direction, three million foreign tourists visited Japan. The most popular destinations are Tokyo, Kyoto, Kanazawa and Beppu.

KARUIZAWA – A HILL RESORT

Karuizawa is a famous resort in the volcanic hills of Honshu. Although it is 150km from Tokyo, good road and rail links mean thousands of people visit as day trippers. It is famous for three attractions:
• its hot springs and traditional hotels
• its cool summer climate and forest walks
• its new winter sports facilities.

B Karuizawa

THE SEAGAIA PHOENIX RESORT

This leisure complex is located on the coast of Miyzaki in southern Kyushu (map **A**).It was opened in 1993 along with a golf course, tennis club, zoo, hotels and convention centre. In its first full year of operation it attracted nearly four million visitors. There is also a fine sandy beach here, but the main attraction is Ocean Dome. The Dome is the biggest indoor water park in the world and can hold up to 10 000 visitors. It is 300m long, 100m wide and 38m high. It has a sliding roof and waves as high as 2.5m can be created.

C Ocean Dome

Developments like this have benefits and costs. They create jobs in rural areas well away from the major cities. But they also have an impact on the environment. Habitats and wildlife are disturbed while large buildings spoil the coastal scenery.

	1965	1975	1985	1995
Japanese leaving	373	2 489	4 024	11 291
Foreigners entering	160	821	1 832	2 855

D Departure and entry of tourists (000s)

Top ten overseas destinations of Japanese tourists (000s)			
USA	3 067	Taiwan	489
South Korea	1 234	China	441
Hong Kong	738	Thailand	313
Australia	594	UK	256
Singapore	553	France	249

Top ten overseas tourists visiting Japan (000s)			
Taiwan	567	Thailand	31
South Korea	397	Brazil	25
USA	214	Hong Kong	23
UK	120	Australia	23
Canada	40	Germany	21

E Overseas tourism

More leisure time is important for the economy as people spend more money on tourism in Japan and overseas (table **D**). This money comes from what people have earned from their jobs in **primary**, **secondary** and **tertiary** activities. It helps create more tertiary jobs, especially in rural and remote areas. This can help reduce **rural migration** to the cities.

FACT FILE

Leisure activities and spending

The table shows the ten most popular leisure activities in Japan in rank order.

1 Dining out
2 Visiting a hot spring
3 Driving
4 Karaoke
5 Drinking in a bar or pub
6 Visiting a zoo, botanical garden, etc.
7 Watching videos
8 Listening to music
9 Visiting an amusement park
10 Lottery

As leisure becomes a more important part of everyday life in Japan, so the amount of money being spent on leisure activities is rising. The proportion of household income now spent on it is 8 per cent. That is more than is spent on medical care. Increased spending on leisure is helping to create still more **tertiary sector** jobs. More facilities are being built. For example, the number of restaurants in Japan has increased by 60 per cent since 1970 and golf practice ranges and golf courses have more than doubled.

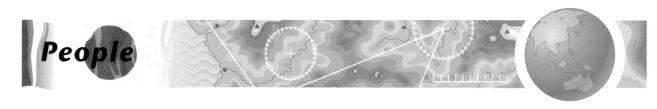

4 HUMAN RESOURCES

People

> ▶ **How have Japanese people made their country so successful?**

Japanese people have a strong national identity and culture. They have their own values, attitudes and codes of behaviour, in spite of the 'westernization' of Japan since 1945. Some characteristics of the Japanese people have been particularly important when it comes to explaining the country's economic success. They have helped make Japan a world superstar and made up for the country's shortage of natural resources.

A A hardworking and conforming labour force

Qualities at work
First, as a rule Japanese people try hard not to be different from each other. What they want most of all is to be accepted and respected as a member of a group. That group may be linked to work, leisure or the home. Belonging to a group gives people a sense of security and well-being (known as *amae*). Being able to work in groups is good for the workplace, as well as for society.

Second, Japanese people believe working hard is a virtue. Everyone is expected to do their best, no matter what their job or status.

Compared with the UK, working hours are longer and leisure time shorter.

There is a tradition that Japanese firms care for their employees. Once a firm has taken workers on they have a job for life. Firms look after their workers, for example by providing housing and medical care, arranging marriages or holidays. In return workers stay loyal and committed to the firm.

Running a business is rather different in Japan. Firms get agreement by involving workers in decisions. There is not a 'them and us' feeling between workers and their bosses. They are part of the same group or team, and team work counts. So strikes are uncommon and there is little need for strong trade unions. Although unemployment has risen, the rate is well below most European countries (table **B** and page 62).

Face
As a people, the Japanese are honest, polite and law-abiding. Part of the reason is that keeping the respect of other people is very important to them. As one Japanese person wrote: 'We are anxious what others think of us, and what we fear most is loss of face'. Keeping **face** has also helped the economy because workers have been prepared to work hard for the sake of Japan.

	Average monthly working hours	Membership of trade union (% of workforce)	Unemployment (% of workforce)
1970	186.6	35.4	0.9
1975	172.0	34.4	1.5
1980	175.7	30.8	1.6
1985	175.8	28.9	2.1
1990	171.0	25.2	3.0

B Some trends at work

WOMEN IN THE WORKFORCE

Sayuri Nakamura is one of Japan's increasing number of working women. There are now over two million of them, but they are still only three per cent of the workforce, compared with 63 per cent in the UK. Sayuri graduated from college fourteen years ago; since then she has worked for a large computer software company. In that time she has married and had two daughters but continued to work.

Sayuri's husband has a job in a publishing company. But because of the cost of housing in Tokyo and of raising a family, they need both incomes. Sayuri has been able to continue her career because her company has a crèche for employees' children. Sayuri's mother lives close by, so she can help with child care.

Nearly three-quarters of Japan's working women are married. Although Japanese society still expects women to quit their job when they start a family, more and more are taking part-time work or continuing their career. So Sayuri is among the first of a new generation in Japan.

C The Nakamura family

FACT FILE

Religion

The main religions in Japan are Shintoism and Buddhism. All but a small percentage of the population follow Shintoism and most of them are also Buddhists. This happens because Shintoism is 'polytheistic' – people who follow Shintoism believe in many gods and there is nothing in it to stop people following another religion as well.

Shintoism is the older religion and grew out of the everyday life of Japanese people in early times. It has a lot to do with fertility, death, the natural world and the seasons. Shinto gods (and there are thousands of them) are worshipped at shrines. People go to a shrine when a child is born or for a wedding. Prayers are said at shrines for various things – for success at work, for help in passing exams or for protection from accidents. But Shintoism has no leaders (such as priests); there are no holy writings (like the Bible) and communal worship (in the form of a service) is rare.

The Japanese have a strong belief in the continuity of life and family ancestors, which is central to Buddhism. The many temples to be found all over Japan are Buddhist.

The Japanese Constitution guarantees religious freedom, so there is no state religion and religious education is forbidden in schools.

Population change

The population of Japan is now about 125 million. People live at an average density of 332 people per km². But in fact only a quarter of Japan's land is suitable for settlement. So its settled areas probably show average densities of over 1000 people per km² – some of the highest in the world.

During the twentieth century, the population of Japan has increased by nearly three times, from 44 to 125 million. The **demographic transition model** helps explain this population growth (graph A). Over the last 100 years Japan has moved from Stage 2 to Stage 4.

Why has the population grown so much?

You can find the answer to this question by investigating birth rates and death rates using graph A. The **birth rate** today is 10 births per 1000 people – less than one-third of what it was in 1900. The reasons for this fall include:
- more birth control
- the high cost of housing
- a more material outlook on life
- a change in thinking about marriage and family life
- more women preferring careers to child-rearing.

As the birth rate has dropped so the average family size has fallen to 3.25. Only half of Japanese households today contain one or more children.

To explain why Japan's population has increased we also need to look at changes in the **death rate**. This has fallen too, from 24 to 6 deaths per 1000 people. The reasons for this include:
- better diet
- improved housing
- healthier environment
- better medical care.

Falling death rates have meant an increase in people's **life expectancy**, especially since 1945. For men it has risen from 65 to 76 years, and for women from 70 to 83 years.

An ageing population

The difference between the birth rate and death rate is called the rate of **natural increase**. In Japan today it is 4 per 1000 people. Although the natural increase rate is a lot lower than in the past, the number of people continues to grow because the total population is much bigger.

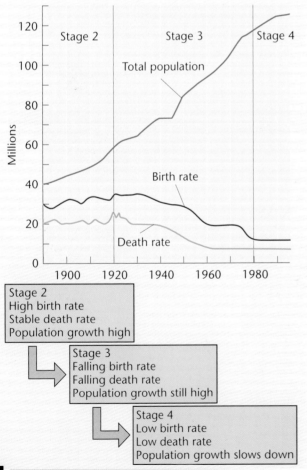

Stage 2
High birth rate
Stable death rate
Population growth high

Stage 3
Falling birth rate
Falling death rate
Population growth still high

Stage 4
Low birth rate
Low death rate
Population growth slows down

The **age-sex pyramid** shows the balance between males and females and the balance between different age groups (diagram **B**). The pyramids show that the Japanese population is gradually getting older; this is sometimes called the 'silvering' of the people (photo **D**).

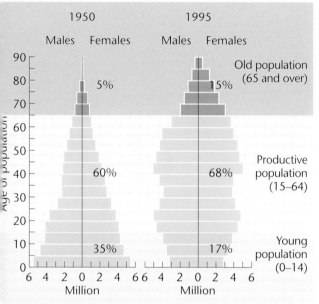

B Japan's changing age–sex pyramid (1950–1995)

D An ageing population

It means that there are more old people who depend on the working population to provide for them, at the same time as the percentage of children is becoming smaller. These changes will have important consequences for Japanese society in the future.

Age	5	10	15	20	25	30	35	40	45	50	55	60	65	70	75	80	85	90
Male (millions)	3.0	3.1	3.5	3.6	3.7	3.5	3.2	3.4	3.7	4.0	5.0	3.7	3.5	3.6	3.6	2.0	1.0	0.5
Female (millions)	2.7	2.8	3.1	3.4	3.4	3.0	2.9	3.0	3.4	4.0	4.7	4.0	3.8	4.0	4.2	3.2	2.0	1.5

C Estimated figures for population in 2025

FACT FILE

Causes of death

At 8 deaths per 1000 population, Japan has one of the lowest death rates in the world. Helping to lower that rate has been better medical care. Since 1981, cancer has been the leading cause of death. The death rate by cancer has risen from 77 per 100 000 population in 1950 to 182 in 1991. Heart disease is the second leading cause of death and is also on the rise. Some think that this is partly due to the change in the Japanese diet, in particular to the eating of more meat and dairy products. Lung disorders have declined a great deal as killers. This may be due to the reduction of atmospheric pollution.

	Male deaths (1991)	Female deaths (1991)
Cancer	143 475	89 252
Heart disease	83 646	85 232
Brain disease	55 740	62 708
Pneumonia and bronchitis	43 372	32 979
Accidents	22 879	10 276
Suicide	12 477	7398
Liver disease	11 438	5476
Tuberculosis	2449	876

A nation of city dwellers

▶ **Why do people live in cities?**
▶ **What are the results of city growth?**

Urbanization

Today, around 80 per cent of Japanese people live in urban areas. Throughout this century, Japanese towns and cities have grown rapidly, a process known as **urbanization**. Until recently, the more towns and cities have grown, the more they have attracted industry, services and yet more people (diagram **A**).

Rural–urban migration

The populations of towns and cities grow in two ways – by **natural increase**, when more people are born than die, and by **rural–urban migration**, when people move in from the countryside. These migrants from rural areas are often young people who may also have children once they have settled in the city. Throughout most of the last 100 years, Japan has experienced massive rural–urban migration. The countryside has been drained of people as cities have mushroomed. Graph **B** shows the speed at which Japan has changed from a rural to an urban society.

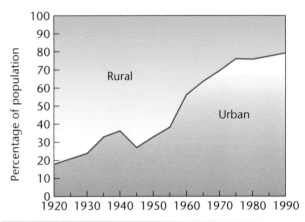

B The urbanization of Japan

The distribution of cities

Japan has eleven cities with over one million people (table **C**). All except one (Sapporo) are located in the Pacific Belt. At the eastern end of the Pacific Belt, four major cities – Tokyo, Yokohama, Kawasaki and Chiba – are so close they have grown together into one huge **metropolitan area**. This wraps around the shores of Tokyo Bay and contains a total population of around 25 million. Two other metropolitan areas have formed from the cities of Osaka, Kyoto and Kobe and from the area around Nagoya. In turn the three metropolitan areas are growing together to form a mammoth elongated urban area called a **megalopolis** (map **D**), stretching from Tokyo to Kobe. Outside Tokaido megalopolis, growth around five other cities (Sapporo, Sendai, Hiroshima and a combined Kitakyushu and Fukuoka) is creating four new metropolitan areas.

Decentralization

Since the 1970s, the rate of urbanization in Japan has slowed down. People and some businesses are now moving out of congested central areas to city suburbs. Some are even moving out of the metropolitan areas to rings of growing commuter towns. Reasons for this **decentralization** include:

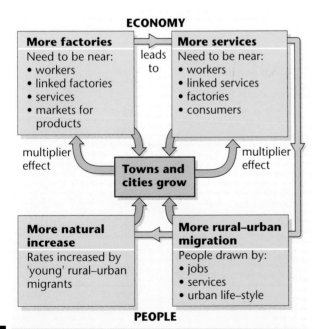

A The multiplier effect: how cities continue to grow

- high costs of city land and buildings
- congestion
- poor quality city environments
- better public transport and communications
- changes in people's taste.

At present, decentralization mainly affects larger cities and is over relatively short distances. This means that concentration of urban growth in the heart of the Pacific Belt looks set to continue in the twenty-first century.

Tokyo	8.1	**Fukuoka**	1.3
Yokohama	3.3	**Kawasaki**	1.2
Osaka	2.6	**Hiroshima**	1.1
Nagoya	2.2	**Kitakyushu**	1.0
Sapporo	1.8	**Sendai**	0.9
Kobe	1.5	**Chiba**	0.8
Kyoto	1.4		

C The major cities of Japan (populations in millions)

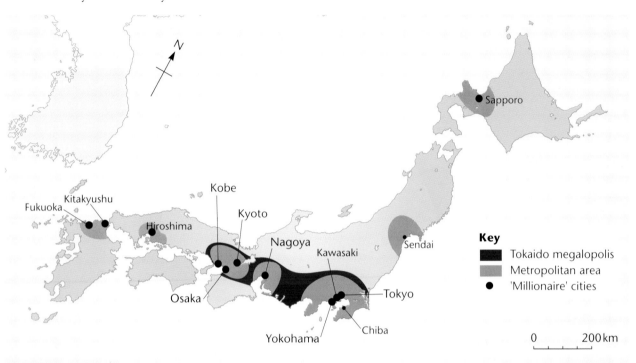

D Japan's megalopolis and metropolitan areas

FACT FILE

Crime

Crime rates in Japan are noticeably lower than in most other developed countries. Tokyo is said to be the safest of the world's major cities. One of the main reasons is that the possession of guns and swords is severely restricted. Another is the Japanese concern about **face** - to be exposed as a criminal would be a serious loss of face. Organized crime (run by gangsters known as the *yakusa*) is mainly to do with prostitution and pornography, fraud and fixing, loans and debt-collection.

Juvenile delinquency has decreased since 1983, when it was at its highest. Violence in schools and in the home, which at one time filled the newspapers in Japan, is falling. So too, is the number of youths arrested for drug offences.

	Crimes per 100 000 population		Arrest rate (%)	
	Murder	Theft	Murder	Theft
Japan	1.0	1226	96.0	30.7
UK	2.5	8135	94.2	22.0
Germany	4.1	4906	90.7	26.9
France	4.7	3607	73.9	12.4
USA	9.3	4903	64.6	17.7

Tokaido megalopolis

▶ Why is the Pacific Belt continuing to grow?
▶ What is it like to live in Tokaido megalopolis?

A Satellite image of Hiroshima, which is likely to become part of Tokaido megalopolis

Benefits and costs

The urban areas of the Pacific Belt continue to grow, attracting industry, business and people. City suburbs fill in the rural spaces between towns and cities, helped by efficient transport links. In this way, that part of the Pacific Belt between Tokyo and Kobe has become linked into a single urban system – Tokaido **megalopolis**. This contains nearly two-thirds of all Japan's population and manufacturing. Most of Japan's specialist services are also found here. If **urbanization** continues, Tokaido megalopolis

will eventually extend further westwards to engulf Hiroshima (photo **A**) and reach as far as Kitakyushu and Fukuoka in northern Kyushu. It will stretch the length of the Pacific Belt. The fast and efficient transport links needed to extend megalopolis in this way already exist.

Why does Tokaido megalopolis continue to grow?

The answer lies in the enormous population and wealth of the Pacific Belt. Industry and services need access to plenty of people, both as workers and customers. In turn as cities prosper and grow, more industry and services grow up to meet the needs of these people and their families. Other industries and services are attracted by **linkages** between businesses, so the region grows still more. An unstoppable upward spiral of growth is created.

Living in Tokaido megalopolis

What is the quality of life like for people living in Tokaido megalopolis? Let us try to answer this question by looking at three different aspects. Next to food, housing is probably the most important. Table **B** compares the housing situation in Tokyo, at the eastern end of Tokaido megalopolis, with that in three other capital cities.

Crime statistics show that Japanese people are law-abiding. The murder rate in Japan is one-sixth of what it is in the UK and mugging is virtually unknown. So people are very safe on the streets of Tokaido megalopolis.

	Tokyo	London	Paris	New York
Average price of residential land (¥1000 per m²)	560	30	29	10
Average house price (¥1000)	132	62	36	33
Area of park per resident (m²)	2.7	23.0	11.6	25.6

B Comparison of housing in four capital cities (¥ = yen – Japanese currency)

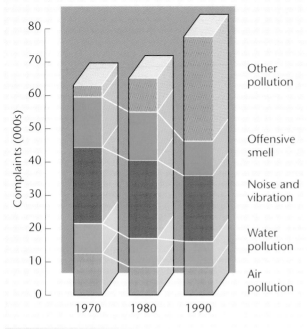

C Pollution complaints

Reducing environmental pollution is only one planning objective in Tokaido megalopolis. Others include:
- improving transport and reducing traffic congestion
- opening up the central areas by lowering land-use densities
- encouraging businesses to move to the suburbs
- improving the quality of housing and services.

Achieving these objectives is made difficult by one basic feature of Tokaido megalopolis – the shortage and high costs of land.

D Congested housing

Since the bad days of the 1960s, much has been done to reduce pollution levels in Tokaido megalopolis. Rivers and coastal waters are now much cleaner, but complaints about other forms of pollution – smell, noise and vibration – remain high (graph **C**). Visual pollution is another feature of Tokaido megalopolis environment – garish advertising, skylines cluttered by pylons and overhead cables disfigure the built environment (photo **D**). Although these forms of pollution may be less damaging to human health than air and water pollution, they do affect personal safety and the quality of life. Congestion, pace and stress are part of everyday life in Tokaido megalopolis. Finding ways of disposing increasing amounts of garbage remains a serious problem.

FACT FILE

The cost of land for housing

A shortage of usable space is one of the major problems of modern Japan. As with any other resource when in short supply, its price goes up. The rise in price has been greatest in the six largest cities. Between 1955 and 1990 the average price of land being sold for housing increased by nearly 2000 times. Since then, however, the price has begun to fall. The government decided to get tough with people speculating in land. As a result, the price of residential land has already fallen by nearly one-third. That is particularly good for people looking for new homes in the suburbs of the largest cities. It not only means cheaper houses, it may also mean a small increase in the average dwelling size.

5 REGIONAL DIFFERENCES

Around the regions

▶ **What are the differences between the regions? What are the similarities?**

Region	% share total area	% mountains	% lowland	Population (millions)	% share total pop.	%share GDP	% share primary sector output	% share secondary sector output	% share tertiary sector output
Hokkaido	22.1	49.0	11.7	5.6	4.6	3.8	10.9	2.6	4.1
Tohoku	17.7	62.0	14.3	9.7	7.8	6.3	16.2	5.3	6.3
Kanto	8.6	40.4	20.7	38.6	31.2	36.6	16.5	35.7	38.3
Chubu	17.7	70.9	14.9	21.0	17.0	17.4	15.9	21.4	15.1
Kinki	8.7	64.1	16.9	22.2	18.0	18.2	8.2	19.5	17.9
Chugoku	8.4	74.1	9.6	7.8	6.3	5.9	6.4	6.2	5.7
Shikoku	5.0	79.9	10.1	4.2	3.4	2.6	6.4	2.3	2.7
Kyushu	11.8	62.7	12.3	14.5	11.7	9.2	19.5	7.0	9.9

B Comparing statistics in the different regions

For the purposes of government, Japan is divided into 47 prefectures. They are the equivalents of the English county and are grouped into eight regions (*chiho*) (map **A**).

Hokkaido
Hokkaido is the most northern island. Its harsh environment and distance from the Pacific Belt make it the most sparsely populated area of Japan. Hokkaido's economy is based on primary activities, especially farming (photo **C**). Tourism is becoming more important.

Tohoku
This is one of five regions on Honshu, the main island. It is another thinly populated part, cut off by mountains. Bullet trains and an expressway have now reduced its remoteness. This is Japan's main rice-growing region. Sendai, a go-ahead city, is a new centre for industry and offices.

Kanto
This region is truly the heart of Japan. It contains Japan's biggest concentration of population. Tokyo, the capital city, is a centre of manufacturing and services. Yokohama is Japan's leading port and Kawaski a major centre of heavy industry. The Kanto plain is important for farming geared to the needs of the huge urban market.

Chubu
This region cuts a section across central Honshu and so has three different parts. Along the Pacific coast, Nagoya is the main city. It is a major centre of the car industry. Inland, large parts of the mountainous area are protected as national parks and produce much of Japan's HEP. On the Japan Sea coast, industry and rice growing are important.

A Regions of Japan

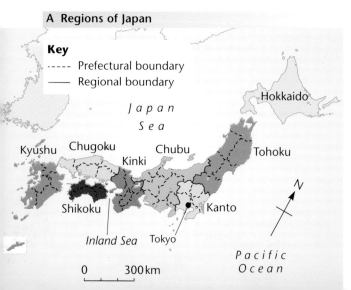

Key
- - - - Prefectural boundary
——— Regional boundary

Japan Sea

Hokkaido

Kyushu Chugoku Chubu Tohoku
Kinki

Shikoku Kanto

Inland Sea Tokyo

N

Pacific Ocean

0   300km

C Hokkaido

Kinki

This is a lowland region containing three major cities: Kyoto, Osaka and Kobe. It is Japan's second most important industrial region.

Chugoku

This small region is in the 'toe' of Honshu. Inland it is mountainous and the Japan Sea coast is remote and undeveloped. But the Inland Sea coast has good transport links and is growing fast. Hiroshima is the main city.

Shikoku

This is the smallest of the main islands. New bridges over the Inland Sea are connecting Shikoku up with Honshu. These will encourage development along the north coast. However the rest of the island is mountainous and remote.

FACT FILE

Prefectures

Japan is divided into 47 prefectures. These are smaller areas within each region. They are not closely tied to the Japanese government. They have considerable freedom in matters such as taxation, law-making and taking initiatives. Individual prefectures can take more decisions for themselves, for example about building a new port or setting up a new university. This freedom of action can be very important for economic growth. The success of individual prefectures' economies is greatly affected by the drive and enterprise of prefectural governments. Prefectural enterprise can often make up for a poor location and a lack of resources.

Kyushu

Kyushu has good transport links with Honshu. The north and south of the island are very different. Two-thirds of the population live in the north of the island, an old industrial area centred on Kitakyushu and Fukuoka. The south is mainly a farming area, but it is also attracting high-tech industry (photo **D**). The south's sub-tropical climate and volcanic scenery attracts tourists.

Japan's regions show similarities and differences. All of them have a mixture of lowland and upland. In all of them the lowlands and coast have attracted settlement and development. However, differences in climate mean differences in farming and living conditions.

D Kyushu

Because prefectural government is so important, the capital of each prefecture has become a significant city. In it are concentrated the various government departments. These, in their turn, attract public and private services as well as many other businesses. These cities stand literally head and shoulders above any other cities within each prefecture.

Core and periphery

▶ Why does a core region develop?
▶ How does the core affect the periphery?

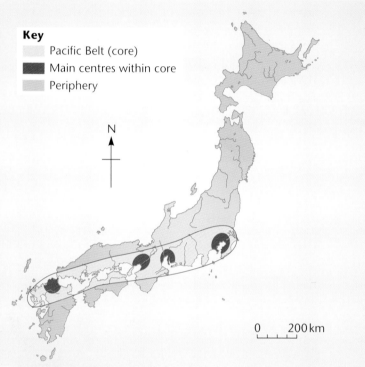

A Japan's core and periphery

B Net migration

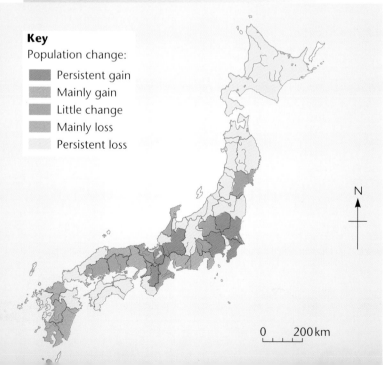

Winners and losers

As we have seen, some parts of Japan are wealthier than others. Kanto, Chubu and Kinki have over 70 per cent of Japan's economic wealth. The other regions produce the remainder, but they make up 65 per cent of the land area. There are economic winners and losers, as in other countries like the UK.

The core

Economic growth in Japan is concentrated in the Pacific Belt, the wealthiest part of the country. This is Japan's economic heart, or **core**. In fact Japan's core region is sausage shaped, stretching from Tokyo round to northern Kyushu. Even the core has its own fastest growing areas, especially around Tokyo (map A).

Advantages and disadvantages of the core

Japan's core first formed around the Inland Sea, which was the best region for settlement, farming, fishing and shipping. This **initial advantage** was enough for the region to get ahead of other parts of Japan. Once the core began to grow, it began to attract more people and economic activities like a magnet. There were many benefits in locating there.

- Being close to other businesses cut down transport costs.
- Businesses could sell their products to the growing, wealthy population.
- The region attracted skilled workers.

The core spread eastwards along the lowlands of the Pacific coast.

There are also costs for businesses and people in the core, for example:

- competition for space means high land prices
- competition for skilled workers leads to higher wages and labour costs
- lack of space leads to congestion, cramped housing and a poor environment
- pressure on the environment leads to pollution of air and water.

All this encourages land reclamation which, in its turn, has environmental costs.

The periphery

The poorer regions outside the core are known as the **periphery**. The main problem for Japan is that as the core grows, it sucks in people and resources from the regions in the periphery. So they lose out while the core gains. It is the loss of population which hurts regions in the periphery most (map **B**). It is usually the younger and more able people who leave. They are attracted to the core by better prospects, for example a better job, higher wages, more services. But once these people leave, they can make things worse for those who are left.

Hope for the periphery

There is some hope for the periphery. People in the booming core region need things that the periphery can supply. People in urban areas need food – this could give Japanese farmers in the periphery the chance to modernize. The countryside of the periphery offers a chance for busy people from the core to escape for leisure and recreation. The core regions also use up huge amounts of energy, while the periphery has empty spaces for nuclear power stations and lakes and rivers for HEP.

FACT FILE

Social class

Although Japan can be divided into core and periphery - prosperous and not so prosperous areas – Japanese society is relatively class-less. Today, the people with high social status are mainly:

- executives in major business companies
- high-level government officials
- professors in the top universities
- professional people – surgeons, lawyers, etc.
- members of the Japanese parliament.

Many people in such positions today started from modest beginnings. In Japan a person's social origins has little to do with their chances of reaching a high social status. Individual effort and achievement in education are the two key factors. There is however one under-privileged group known as the *burakumin* or *eta*. Historically, this class of outcasts were made up of people making their living from the slaughter of livestock and the working of leather. Today the class also includes prostitutes, beggars and tramps.

LAND RECLAMATION

Because of the shortage of space, the Japanese have had to create land themselves, especially by **reclaiming** land from the sea. In Tokyo Bay, over 100 000 hectares of new land have been reclaimed. The size of the Bay has been reduced by pushing out the shoreline and by creating huge artificial islands in the bay (map **C**). The new land has been used to extend the port and Haneda airport, as well as for industry, new offices and housing and leisure complexes. The costs are enormous but developers are willing to pay the price, especially around Tokyo and other big cities where the demand for space is highest.

C Tokyo Bay land reclamation

Transport and accessibility

Good transport links are very important in Japan. Good **accessibility** is needed because:
- Japan is a nation of islands which need to be linked
- three-quarters of the country is mountainous
- population and industry are located on separate small lowlands around the coast.

Rail network (shinkansen lines)

Road network (expressways)

A Most major transport networks

Rail transport

Japan is famous for its high-speed passenger **bullet trains** (*shinkansen*). There are three lines out of Tokyo – to Fukuoka, Morioka and Niigata (map A). These are being extended and made even faster. In towns and cities, underground and suburban trains play an important part in getting commuters to work.

LINKING THE ISLANDS

Before 1942 the four main islands were only connected by ferry services. Since then, with government backing, a number of bridges and tunnels have been built to link the islands. Some of these are spectacular feats of engineering.

The first direct links by tunnel and suspension bridge were built between Honshu and Kyushu. Hokkaido and Honshu are now linked by the Seikan rail tunnel, the longest tunnel in the world.

The Inland Sea is being crossed by three bridge links from Shikoku to Honshu (photo **B**). The bridges use small islands as stepping stones. All of them have two tiers, one for road and one for rail. The bridge across the Akashi Straits to Kobe will be the longest in the world. But the recent Kobe earthquake moved the bridge over a metre to the west.

B One of Shikoku's new bridges

Road transport

There are now over 60 million vehicles on Japan's roads, 39 million of them cars. In cities many people use cars for commuting in spite of public transport. Car use is increasing and traffic congestion is often severe (table C). Outside cities, Japan's mountains and islands make road-building difficult. There is really only one national expressway, from Aomori in northern Honshu to Kagoshima in southern Kyushu (map A).

Air transport
Air transport within Japan is not important compared with road and rail. It is used mainly to move people, as well as some high-value

	1970	1980	1993
Passengers (% of total)			
Rail	40.4	34.8	27.7
Road	29.1	19.1	10.0
Car	30.1	45.7	62.1
Air	0.0	0.0	0.1
Ship	0.4	0.3	0.2
Freight (% of total)			
Rail	4.9	2.7	1.2
Road	88.0	88.9	90.5
Ship	7.2	8.4	8.2

C Domestic transport (1970–93)

KANSAI INTERNATIONAL AIRPORT

This was opened in 1994. It is located in Osaka Bay and was built 5km from the coast on land reclaimed from the sea. Although Kansai airport is on an artificial island it still has very good transport links. A jet foil service runs from Kobe and there is a bridge to the mainland for express road and rail services. Aviation fuel is brought in by tanker to a special jetty.

D Aerial view of Kansai airport

goods like microchips and flowers. By contrast international air travel is booming. The volume of traffic is so great that Tokyo has two international airports, with four others in other parts of Japan.

Summing up
Japan has invested huge amounts of money in improving transport links. Modern transport is needed to link the lowlands together, and to link the more remote **periphery** with the **core** region. The hope is that better accessibility will encourage economic growth in the periphery. The bad news is that traffic congestion is a serious problem in many parts of the core.

FACT FILE
Commuting
Most Japanese cities have strong central areas, in which jobs and services are highly concentrated. This concentration, in turn, leads to huge daily movements of people from their homes in the suburbs and outlying settlements into central-city areas. In Tokyo, the daily volume of passengers travelling into the central area is more than two million. A great strain is put on city transport networks. Severe traffic jams are part of everyday city life. The largest cities look to the railways to help solve the problem. Underground systems have the advantage of not using much surface space, but they are very expensive to build.

Japan's major subway (underground) systems (1994)

	Operating distance (km)	Number of lines	Passengers carried daily (thousands)
Tokyo	230	12	9037
Osaka	106	7	2667
Nagoya	77	6	1402
Sapporo	40	3	748

Three prefectures

▶ **What contrasts are there between prefectures in different parts of Japan?**

Here we take a closer look at three **prefectures** located in different parts of Japan. The three show inequalities in wealth and in their future prospects. One is part of Japan's **core**; the other two are in the **periphery**.

These three prefectures show basic differences in geography and development. The difference in development is largely the result of differences in distance from the core.

	Chiba	Miyagi	Kochi
Total area (km^2)	5 081	6 860	7 104
Mountains (%)	8	31	86
Urban area (%)	29	7	5
Population (1990)	5 550 000	2 249 000	825 000
Population change (1980–90)	+79 100	+33 000	–17 500
Manufacturing (% total employed)	21	17	12
Services (% total employed)	71	68	67
GDP (¥billion)	16	7	2

A Comparative statistics for three prefectures

CHIBA PREFECTURE

Chiba prefecture

Chiba is on the eastern side of Tokyo Bay. It forms the eastern limit of Japan's core – the Pacific Belt. Recent suburban growth along railway lines and main roads has joined it to the Tokyo metropolitan area and so to Tokaido megalopolis.

Many of the working people **commute** into Tokyo. On land reclaimed from the Bay, there is a fringe of waterfront industries, such as oil-refining, petrochemicals and iron and steel. There is also housing on this land. Port facilities have been built to allow the import of oil and raw materials and the export of manufactured goods. Narita Airport is Japan's leading international airport. It was built in the 1970s amid much public protest. Local people were angry about the clearance of over 1000 homes, the loss of farmland and the great increase in noise.

The prospects for this prosperous prefecture are good. But there are challenges, such as making sure that future growth does not cause congestion or too much damage to the environment.

B Tokyo Bay waterfront

C Location of the three prefectures

MIYAGI PREFECTURE

This is one of the few prefectures in the Japanese periphery now enjoying economic growth and rising prosperity. It is part of Japan's main rice-producing region. Improvement of transport has been the key fact in turning round the fortunes of Miyagi. Travel times over the 300km or so from Tokyo have been reduced to a few hours. A new port has been built at Shiogama. This better **accessibility** has encouraged the setting up of new industries and offices in and around the city of Sendai. If Miyagi continues to grow it could become part of Japan's core. In the meantime the challenge is to try and spread future growth more evenly across the prefecture.

D Sendai – a dynamic centre in Miyagi in the Japanese periphery

KOCHI PREFECTURE

This prefecture, in southern Shikoku, is made up of a long coastal plain surrounded by mountains. Although there are now bridges linking Shikoku to Honshu, this part of the island remains cut off from the rest of the country. Things are beginning slowly to change. Instead of growing two crops of rice each year, farmers are now exploiting the warm climate by producing early vegetables, fruit and flowers for the major urban markets of the Pacific Belt. Improvement of the Kochi airport would help. It would also help attract more tourists to this quiet and unspoilt corner of the country. But will it do anything to halt the loss of population from the prefecture? One problem is that the Kochi coast is the part of Japan most exposed to **typhoons** sweeping in from the Pacific.

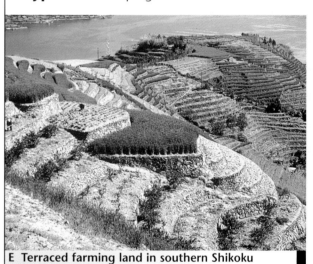

E Terraced farming land in southern Shikoku

FACT FILE
Economic indicators (1990)

	Chiba	Miyagi	Kochi
Rice production (000 tons)	343	484	74
Working forest (000 ha)	0.9	3.1	4.0
Fish catches (000 tons)	372	593	149
Iron and steel output (¥ billion)	1629	133	24
Electrical goods (¥ billion)	1142	812	16
Processed food (¥ billion)	980	613	65
Retail sales (¥ billion)	4474	1166	731
Motor vehicles owned (000)	2326	1088	434
Housing land (¥000 per m²)	268	61	46
Primary school teachers	18 477	8445	4060
Hospital beds (000s)	50.4	25.3	21.8
Local taxes (¥ billion)	689 652	237 907	67 917

Trade

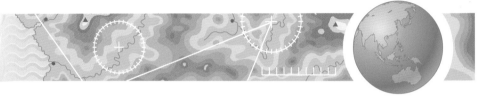

▶ **Why is international trade so important to Japan?**
▶ **How have Japan's exports and imports changed?**

Overseas trade is selling and buying with other countries. It is a two-way traffic. For example, Japan makes cars and sells them abroad (**exports**). To make more cars raw materials and energy are needed, so the money is used to buy these from other countries (**imports**).

Exports
Exports are goods or services that Japan sells to other countries. The Japanese economy is so strong it creates around ten per cent of all world exports. Exports have changed a lot since 1955 as Japanese industry has changed (table B). The biggest growth has been in machinery and equipment. This includes the **consumer goods** for which Japan is world famous, such as cars, electrical and electronic goods.

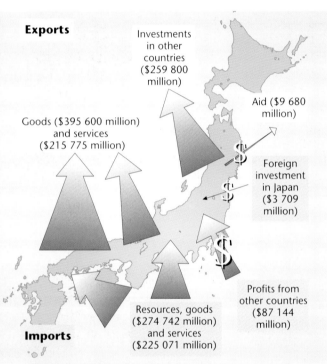

Exports

Investments in other countries ($259 800 million)

Aid ($9 680 million)

Goods ($395 600 million) and services ($215 775 million)

Foreign investment in Japan ($3 709 million)

Profits from other countries ($87 144 million)

Resources, goods ($274 742 million) and services ($225 071 million)

Imports

A Japan's international economy

Japan's international economy
Japan's economy today is truly global. There are few parts of the world that do not have some contact with Japan. Developing an international economy has helped make it one of the wealthiest countries in the world. Through the three links of trade, investment and aid, Japan is able to:
• obtain **resources**
• reach foreign markets
• make profits
• gain economic influence in other parts of the world (map A).

Through these links the economy draws more of its energy and strength from abroad.

Exports	1955	1965	1975	1985	1995
Machinery and equipment	12.4	42.1	61.3	71.8	76.0
Metals	19.2	13.9	17.8	10.5	6.1
Chemicals	5.1	6.5	5.9	4.4	6.0
Textile products	37.3	16.3	5.1	3.6	2.1
Other manufactures	19.7	17.6	8.9	8.9	9.3
Foodstuffs	6.3	3.6	1.0	0.8	0.5
Imports					
Foodstuffs	25.3	18.0	15.2	12.0	17.0
Raw materials	51.1	39.4	20.2	13.9	10.4
Mineral fuels	11.7	19.9	44.3	30.9	17.4
Manufactured goods	11.9	22.7	20.3	43.2	55.2

B The changing make-up of exports and imports (%)

Imports

Imports are **goods** that Japan buys from other countries. They are mainly things Japan cannot produce itself, such as oil and other raw materials. Changes in industry mean Japan today imports less fuel and raw materials than in the past.

The balance of trade

Japan's success in selling its goods overseas is shown in the **balance of trade**, the difference between exports and imports. Japan's exports are valued at $120 billion more than its imports, a huge trade surplus. With some of Japan's trading partners the surplus is so large it causes ill feeling, known as **trade friction**. Some trading partners threaten to protect themselves by making it more difficult for Japan to export to them.

Japan also trades in services, such as international transport and travel, investment, research and development. Here, Japan imports more services than it exports, and so has a small trade deficit of $10 billion. However, overall Japan has a favourable **balance of payments**.

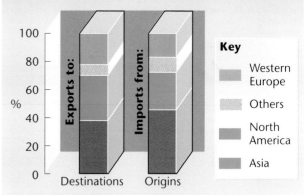

C Destinations and origins of trade in goods

Key:
- Western Europe
- Others
- North America
- Asia

	Exports %	Imports%
Hong Kong	6.5	0.8
South Korea	6.2	4.9
Taiwan	6.0	3.9
Singapore	5.0	1.7
China	4.5	10.0
Thailand	3.7	3.0
Malaysia	3.1	3.0
Indonesia	1.9	4.7
Philippines	1.5	1.0
India	0.5	1.0
Vietnam	0.1	0.5
Others	0.8	10.6
ASIA	38.8	45.1

D Japan's exports and imports for Asia (1994)

FACT FILE

The value of the yen

One of the clearest measures of Japan's economic success has been the increase in the value of its currency - the yen. The table shows just how much the yen has 'appreciated' (increased in value) against the US dollar. Today, the Japanese yen challenges the US dollar as the world's most important currency.

The increasing value of the yen has been a mixed blessing for Japan. On the one hand, a strong yen buys more. This helps imports. On the other hand, a strong yen makes exporting more difficult, because more foreign currency is needed to buy Japanese goods. Japanese goods become more expensive.

Year	US dollar exchange rate (yen)
1960	362
1965	361
1970	358
1975	297
1980	227
1985	239
1990	145
1995	101

Overseas investment and aid

▶ How and why does Japan invest abroad?

Trade, overseas investment and aid are three ways the Japanese economy is becoming more international. Overseas investment can happen in three ways:

- setting up **branch factories** and **branch offices** in other countries, e.g. Sony's factories in the UK
- agreeing **joint ventures** to share technology and ideas, e.g. Rover in the UK and Honda
- putting money into overseas companies so as to influence what they do.

Japan's overseas investment is huge and is growing every year. Much of it is made by giant firms like Mitsubishi and Matsushita. Today something like 70 per cent goes to North America and Europe, with the USA and the UK the main targets (graph **A**). By setting up branch factories in these countries, Japanese firms can produce goods locally rather than exporting them from Japan. So they cut down on transport costs and customs duties. It is important to remember that far more of Japanese overseas investment is to do with services rather than manufacturing.

Aid

Aid is the third overseas economic link. Japan is proud of its record of giving aid. It gives 0.3 per cent of its **Gross National Product** (GNP), about the same as the UK. Some goes to organizations like the United Nations, the rest goes directly to over 130 countries, mainly in Asia, especially China, Indonesia, the Philippines and Thailand (graph **B**). This direct aid takes two forms:

- grants of money and technical help from Japan
- loans for major projects, such as transport improvements.

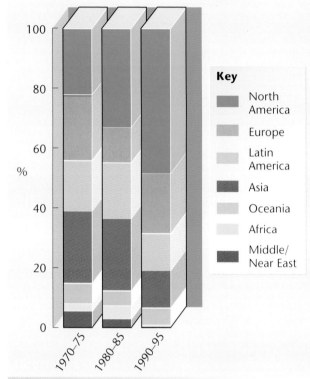

A Japanese overseas investment

Key
- North America
- Europe
- Latin America
- Asia
- Oceania
- Africa
- Middle/Near East

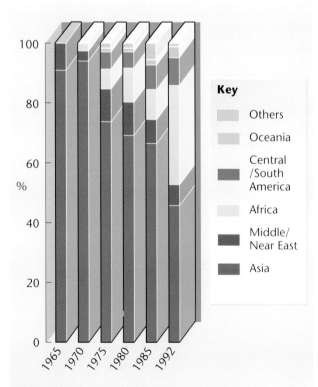

B Japanese aid

Key
- Others
- Oceania
- Central/South America
- Africa
- Middle/Near East
- Asia

AID TO CHINA

In 1995 China took a fifteen per cent share of Japan's direct aid, more than any other country. It was worth $1.5 billion. Much of the aid is in the form of loans. It is being used to help complete major projects. These include new ports, HEP stations, a modern communications network, modernizing factories and new oil and coalfields.

Why does Japan give aid to China? Why should a small **capitalist** country be helping a huge **communist** one? Japan needs a good relationship with China because Japan is China's biggest foreign investor and China is now Japan's second most important trading partner. Japan needs access to China's oil and coal supplies. Japan also wants to be able to sell goods to China's millions of consumers. So both Japan and China gain from the aid.

Over half of direct aid is in the form of loans from Japan. The problem with loans is they have to be repaid and interest is charged on them. Loans can easily drive poorer countries into debt.

Aid can help countries improve people's quality of life. But some projects are useful for Japanese companies too, for example the building of a new port or railway line. These projects could be seen as helping Japanese companies exploit new sources of energy or raw materials, as well as helping local people.

C A major aid project in China

FACT FILE

Overseas investment and aid - some international comparisons

	Overseas investment ($ million)		Aid	
	Outward	Inward	Total ($ million)	Ratio to GNP (%)
Japan	259.8	16.9	13 240	0.29
France	167.1	130.3	8450	0.64
Germany	184.7	123.5	6750	0.33
UK	258.7	196.3	3090	0.30
USA	548.6	445.3	9850	0.15

Overseas investment in Japan	% of all investment
USA	40.4
Netherlands	8.2
Switzerland	6.3
Germany	5.5
Canada	4.8
UK	4.5
Hong Kong	2.1

The economic links between Japan and the UK

▶ **Why has Japan invested in the UK?**
▶ **Has it benefited the UK?**

Although Japan does more business with the USA than any other country, the UK is Japan's main partner in Europe. There are two main economic links – trade and investment.

Trade
People in the UK are very aware that many household goods are made by Japanese companies, for example Sony, Mitsubishi and Nissan. But Japanese goods in the shops are

A Japanese Panasonic factory in South Wales

just an example of trade between the two countries. Goods like Wedgewood china and Scotch whiskey are bought by Japan's wealthy and fashion-loving consumers.

Trade between Japan and the UK has winners and losers. The UK loses out on trade in **goods**; Japan's **exports** to the UK are twice as valuable as the UK's exports to Japan. But the UK wins on other trade, for example tourism and services (table **D**). Overall, the losses are roughly balanced by the gains. But because trade in goods is much more obvious some people believe the UK should cut **imports** from Japan.

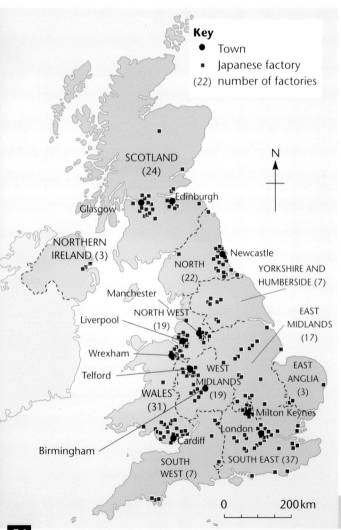

Key
- ● Town
- ■ Japanese factory
- (22) number of factories

SCOTLAND (24)
Edinburgh
Glasgow
NORTHERN IRELAND (3)
Newcastle
NORTH (22)
YORKSHIRE AND HUMBERSIDE (7)
Manchester
NORTH WEST (19)
Liverpool
EAST MIDLANDS (17)
Wrexham
Telford
WEST MIDLANDS (19)
EAST ANGLIA (3)
WALES (31)
Milton Keynes
London
Cardiff
Birmingham
SOUTH WEST (7)
SOUTH EAST (37)

N

0   200 km

B The distribution of Japanese branch factories in the UK

Investment in manufacturing

The first Japanese factory in the UK was built in 1972. Since then nearly 300 branch factories have been built creating around 70 000 jobs (photo **A**). **Branch factories** have been set up to make goods locally, rather than importing them from Japan. There are several advantages for Japanese firms.
- They make the trade figures with Japan look better (**trade friction** is reduced).
- They save on transport costs.
- Factories in the UK can take advantage of free trade to sell to other countries in the European Union (EU).

Japanese factories in the UK make a wide range of **consumer goods**. As well as cars and electronics, they make things like zips and fishing tackle. The distribution of Japanese factories in the UK is uneven (map **B**). Many have been set up in 'assisted areas' like the North-East where the UK Government, the EU and local authorities give help to new investors. About one third of all Japanese manufacturing investment in the EU ends up in the UK. Some of the reasons can be seen in graph **C**.

Investment in services

Japanese people are great savers and investors. Recently they have put large sums of money into banks, property and other investments in the UK. In fact the Japanese have put twice as much money into UK services as they have in factories. The UK is attractive to investors in Japan because:
- London is one of the world's main centres of finance
- the UK is a safe place to keep your money – there is little risk.

	Goods ($million)	Services ($million)
Exports from Japan to UK	12 734	32 840
Imports from UK to Japan	5 914	41 910

D Japanese exports and imports for the UK

FACT FILE

The growth of Japanese branch factories in the UK

Year	New factories or expansions	Jobs created
Before 1980	13	7388
1980	3	616
1981	2	1330
1982	4	1703
1983	3	1430
1984	4	1591
1985	7	9045
1986	9	1621
1987	19	7096
1988	22	4757
1989	24	6715
1990	20	6548
1991	19	3878
1992	20	3352
1993	23	3878
1994	18	3484

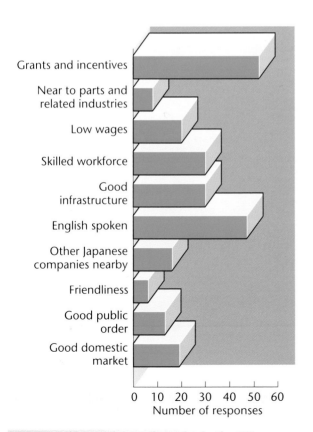

Grants and incentives
Near to parts and related industries
Low wages
Skilled workforce
Good infrastructure
English spoken
Other Japanese companies nearby
Friendliness
Good public order
Good domestic market

0 10 20 30 40 50 60
Number of responses

C Reasons for setting up factories in the UK

Japan and the environment

▶ What has Japan achieved at home?
▶ How has its economic growth affected the global environment?

Achievements at home

Japan has done much to reduce pollution and improve the quality of the environment. The Japanese people are now much more aware of the need to protect and conserve habitats and wildlife. But there are still some problems to be solved. These include:

- reducing damage caused by land reclamation to habitats

- finding good ways of disposing of garbage – recycling can only do so much
- improving the design of urban environments
- imposing even tighter controls on exhaust emissions from motor vehicles.

The global environment

Since Japan's economy has become international, Japan's economic growth has affected environments outside the country.

JAPAN AND THE SEA

Japan has been reluctant to observe the international ban on commercial whaling. Whale meat has always been a delicacy in Japan and it still appears on shop-counters in Tokyo. How?

Japan's fishing fleets operate in the international waters of all the oceans. Accusations are often made about their methods and equipment, for example, size of nets, fineness of mesh. Are they really concerned about conservation of global fish stocks?

A Japan continues to hunt whales

JAPAN AND THE TROPICAL RAINFOREST

Japan is the world's largest consumer of tropical hardwoods. Japan imports tropical timber from Brazil and SE Asia, especially the Philippines, Thailand, Indonesia, Malaysia and Cambodia. Japan consumes huge quantities of softwoods from Siberia and N America. Japan has hard and softwoods of its own. Why is it not harvesting these rather than felling other people's forests? Better still, why is it not using its modern technology to come up with alternative materials?

B Timber from Malaysian rainforest which has been imported to Japan

EXPORTING POLLUTION?

Japanese overseas investment and aid have been setting up industrial projects in developing countries. Some projects involve the refining and smelting of metal ores as, for example in Brazil (photo **C**) and Indonesia. Is it just coincidence that these industries were among the worst polluters of Japan's environment during the 1960s? They are now subject to very strong anti-pollution control in Japan. Another example is nuclear waste which Japan ships to the UK for reprocessing. So it is possible that Japan 'exports' its pollution through these projects.

C A metal smelter at Carajas in Brazil

ACID RAIN FROM CHINA

As the economic boom sweeps across China, Chinese factories are producing record levels of pollution. In 1995, Japanese scientists reported that the area of Japan affected by acid rain from Chinese factories had increased by 7.5 times in two years. More than 280 000km^2 had been damaged by the pollution.

Government officials from Japan and China have met to find ways of dealing with the problem. One solution offered by the Japanese is to build an environmental research centre in Beijing. At a local level, Kitakyshu, at one time renowned as the most polluted city in Japan, has received government aid to help the Chinese city of Dairen to improve its environment.

In 1996 the Environmental Agency reported that the level of nitrogen dioxide in the air over Japan was the highest in ten years. It also warned that the **ozone layer** over Hokkaido had decreased by 30 per cent in some places. The cause of this destruction was traced to clouds of nitric acid in the air – clouds many claim originated in China.

Maybe Japan is guilty of not doing enough to ensure a sustainable use of the world's resources. Like most nations, it could also do more to protect the global environment.

Actions always speak louder than words. But there are also examples where Japan is the victim of the carelessness of other nations. When it comes to pollution, the fact is no country is an island.

FACT FILE

Who is responsible for the environment?
Japan's official environmental organization is the Environmental Agency set up in 1971. Because it is an agency of the Prime Minister's Office rather than a ministry, it lacks their status and influence. Its two main tasks are pollution control and nature conservation.

Compared with the UK, the membership of non-government organizations is small. This is particularly true of Japan's branches of western-style pressure groups such as Friends of the Earth, Greenpeace or the World Wide Fund for Nature. The Japanese preference for cooperation rather than confrontation may be partly the

reason. However, the Japanese have shown keen and active support for local environmental schemes, such as recycling garbage, cleaning up rivers or setting up small nature reserves.

Overseas, the Japanese government is keen to take the lead in high-profile events such as the 1992 UN Conference on Environment and Development (the 'Earth Summit' as it has been called). Part of Japan's aid programme provides loans for pollution control and for treating environmental damage. However, it is Japan's consumer demands for fish, timber and other environmental products that continue to threaten the global environment.

Issues for the twenty-first century

▶ What is the future for Japan and the Asian Pacific region?

As the year 2000 approaches, all nations are thinking more than usual about their futures. In Japan there are three sorts of issues to think about:
• those that are to do with the situation inside Japan
• those that are about Japan and its relationships with other countries, particularly in the Asian Pacific region
• those that are to do with Japan and the Asian Pacific region as a whole.

ISSUES IN JAPAN

1   The Japanese people have come to expect rising wealth and prosperity. But can an economy that has moved **offshore** and is based more on services keep producing more wealth?

2   Can Japan provide the services and support needed for its ageing population?

3   What can be done to improve housing, the environment and the quality of life?

4   Will Japan's **core** region continue to grow at the expense of the **periphery**?

5   Japan is already an economic superstar. Should it become more of a world political leader?

JAPAN AND THE ASIAN PACIFIC REGION AS A WHOLE

1   Should Japan speak up more in the politics of the region?

2   Would Japan benefit from setting up a free trade area in the Asian Pacific region (perhaps like the European Union)?

3   Would it be useful to set up a free trade area right around the Pacific Ocean?

JAPAN AND THE COMMUNIST COUNTRIES

1   Should political differences stop Japan from cooperating with these countries?

2   Can Japan encourage their economies to become more market–orientated (**capitalist**)?

3   How good are the economic opportunities in these countries? Should Japan try to exploit them?

4   Will China replace Japan as the number one economy of the Asian Pacific region, and when?

JAPAN AND THE ASIAN TIGERS

1 How can Japan fight off competition from these countries?

2 Will they overtake Japan as regional leaders?

3 Can Japan cooperate more with them, for example in investment, research and development?

4 Should Japan be doing more to support Taiwan and South Korea? Remember that China still claims Taiwan and there is continuing hostility between South and North Korea.

5 Will Hong Kong still be in competition with Japan now that it has returned to Chinese rule?

JAPAN AND THE LOWER MIDDLE INCOME ECONOMIES

1 Should Japan do more to help development in these countries?

2 Should Japan change the type of aid, shifting the emphasis from loans to grants and the transfer of technology?

3 What should Japan do to ensure it uses resources from these countries in a sustainable way?

4 These countries have low wages, raw materials and energy resources. What sort of competition could they be for Japan, and how soon?

5 Could there be more partnership between Japan and these countries?

FACT FILE

Defence
The Peace Treaty of 1951 and the Japanese Constitution do not allow Japan to threaten or use military force to settle international disputes. The international community that drew up the Constitution were determined that Japan should never again become a military power. Since the end of the Second World War, much of Japan's defence has been provided by the USA. It has been keen to protect Japan from invasion by **communist** troops from China or the former Soviet Union. Its strategic location as a base for stopping the spread of communism was also too valuable to lose.

Japan is now allowed a self-defence force which includes 1180 tanks, 61 destroyers and 289 fighter planes. For the last 20 years the Japanese have kept their spending on this self-defence force to about one per cent of GNP. This is much lower than in most countries.

Statistics

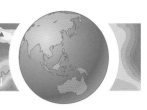

	UK	ITALY	BRAZIL	JAPAN	INDIA
Total area (km²)	244 100	301 270	8 511 965	377 801	3 287 260
Total population (millions)	58.3	57.2	159.1	125.2	943.0
Population density: people per km²	241	194	19	332	317

Population

	UK	ITALY	BRAZIL	JAPAN	INDIA
Birth rate per 1000 people	14	11	26	10	31
Death rate per 1000 people	12	11	8	6	10
Life expectancy (male and female)	73M 79F	73M 80F	64M 69F	76M 83F	60M 61F
Fertility (children per female)	2	1	3	2	4
Population structure 0–14 15–59 60+	19% 60% 21%	17% 63% 20%	35% 58% 7%	19% 64% 17%	37% 56% 7%
Urban population	89%	67%	76%	77%	26%

Environment and economy

	UK	ITALY	BRAZIL	JAPAN	INDIA
Rate of urban growth per year	0.3%	0.6%	2.3%	0.6%	2.9%
Land use: arable grass forest	27% 46% 10%	31% 17% 23%	7% 22% 58%	11% 2% 67%	56% 4% 23%
% of workforce in: farming industry services	2 28 70	9 32 59	25 25 50	7 34 59	62 11 27
GNP per person (US$)	$17 970	$19 620	$2 920	$31 450	$290
Unemployment	9.4%	11.6%	5.9%	3.0%	n/a
Energy used (tonnes/person/year)	5.40	4.02	0.44	4.74	0.35

Society and quality of life

	UK	ITALY	BRAZIL	JAPAN	INDIA
Infant mortality (deaths per 1000 births)	8	9	57	5	88
People per doctor	300	211	1000	600	2439
Food supply (calories per person per day)	3317	3561	2824	2903	2395
Adult literacy	99%	97%	81%	99%	50%
TVs per 1000 people	434	421	207	613	35
Aid received or given per person	$50 given	$53 given	$1.2 received	$90 given	$1.7 received
Education spending (% of GNP)	5.3	4.1	n/a	5.0	3.5
Military spending (% of GNP)	4.0	2.0	n/a	1.0	2.5
United Nations Human Development Index (out of 1.0)	0.92	0.91	0.80	0.94	0.44

Figures are for 1992–95. Source: *Philip's Geographical Digest* (United Nations, World Bank). The Human Development Index is worked out by the UN. It is a summary of national income, life expectancy, adult literacy and education. It is a measure of human progress. In 1992, HDI ranged from 0.21 to 0.94.

General

Longest river: Shinano river (367km)
Highest mountain: Fuji (3776m)
Largest lake: Biwa (670.5 km^2)
Largest city: Tokyo (8.1 million)
Capital: Tokyo
Languages: Japanese
Currency: Yen
Religion: Shinto (40%), Buddhist (38%),
Christian (4%)

Economic

Japan's leading manufactured goods (1993)

Value of production (¥ trillion)	
Electrical goods	17.82
Metals	16.83
Food	15.15
General machinery (e.g. office and power generating equipment)	14.04
Transport equipment (e.g. ships, motor vehicles)	12.99
Chemicals	10.32
Oil and coal products	5.40
Ceramics and cement	4.39
Pulp and paper	3.51
Textiles	2.41
Precision instruments	1.72

Ownership of household goods, 1995

	% of households	
	Japan	UK
Colour TV	98.9	97
Video recorder	73.7	72
Computer	39.4	23
Video camera	31.3	10*
Washing machine	99.3	90
Microwave oven	84.3	70
Refrigerator with freezer	97.9	86
Fax machine	10.0	n/a
Piano	23.3	n/a
Car	82.1	69

*estimate only

Social

Internal migration

	Japanese living overseas	Foreigners living in Japan
Argentina	11 830	n/a
Australia	21 452	6219
Brazil	92 615	159 619
Canada	23 756	6883
China	13 675	218 585
Germany	22 908	n/a
Hong Kong	18 528	n/a
Peru	n/a	33 169
Philippines	n/a	85 968
Singapore	21 296	n/a
South Korea	9197	676 793
Thailand	20 804	13 997
UK	45 617	12 453
USA	256 157	43 320

Communications and media (1993)

	Mail (posted letters per person)	Tele-phones (per 1000 people)	TV sets (per 1000 people)	Daily news-papers (per 1000 people)
Japan	196	464	281	576
Australia	220	487	475	n/a
UK	287	446	360	383
USA	664	515	927	240

Glossary

accessibility how easily a place may be reached

age–sex pyramid a diagram showing the structure of a population in terms of age and sex

archipelago a group of islands

assisted area an area receiving aid from the government to halt its decline or to encourage development

balance of trade the difference in the value of goods exported and goods imported. If exports are larger than imports, then the balance is described as 'favourable'

balance of payments the difference between a country's total amount of money received from other countries and the amount of money paid to other countries

birth rate the number of births in a year per 1000 of total population

branch plant a factory or office set up by a company because of increased business. Often located well away from the main factory or headquarters, perhaps overseas

bullet train the name given to the *shinkansen* – Japan's high-speed train

capitalist an economy or society based on private enterprise, i.e. individuals rather than the government or state

communist an economy or society run by the state

commute to travel daily to and from work

components parts which make up the whole of something, e.g. a computer

consumer goods a range of products – from food to furniture, clothes to cars – used by people in daily life

continental climate a type of climate found near centres of large land masses; temperatures are extreme in summer and winter and precipitation is low

cooperative a group sharing equipment and acting together, e.g. farmers when buying seeds, fertilizers, etc., and selling produce

core a favoured and successful area in which people, jobs and services become concentrated

death rate the number of deaths in a year per 1000 of total population

decentralization the outward movement of people, jobs and services within and away from cores and cities

demographic transition model a simplified diagram showing how birth and death rates and therefore population growth change over time. There are four different stages in the model

diversify to introduce new activities and products and so broaden the range

dormant a volcano that is inactive but not dead

exports goods and services sold to foreign countries

face the character and behaviour of a person as seen by others

fold mountains an upland area formed by the buckling of the Earth's crust

geothermal energy energy extracted from the Earth's natural heat, i.e. from hot springs and certain kinds of rock

goods any objects or products that meet the needs of people

gross domestic product (GDP) the total value of goods produced and services provided in a nation during one year

gross national product (GNP) the GDP of a nation plus any money earned from overseas investment and minus any money paid to people from overseas

hazard perception the way in which people see and react to natural events of a hazardous nature

high-tech industry manufacturing using the latest technology; it includes making microchips, computers, industrial robots, telecommunications, fibre optics and new materials

human resources those features of people, such as their number, hard work, skills and enterprise, that are used in the process of development

humid subtropical climate the warm and moist climate found in areas just outside the tropics

hydrograph a graph which shows the changes in a river's flow over time

imports goods and services bought from a foreign country

initial advantage something which gives one area an advantage over another. It might be a good location or climate, fertile soil or mineral deposits

input something that is used or processed in production

invisible trade trade in services, research and money

island arc a line of islands

joint venture an arrangement where two companies agree to share things such as research, production, management and marketing

land reclamation the creation of new land by draining marshes, lakes and shallow parts of the sea

levee the raised bank of a river built up during flooding

life expectancy the average number of years a person may expect to live

linkage a connection between businesses involved in the same industry or service

market economy a capitalist economy in which production, distribution and exchange are carried out by private companies and individuals rather than by the state

megalopolis a vast urban settlement created by the growing together of metropolitan areas and cities that were once separate

metropolitan area a large city and its surrounding suburbs and commuter settlements

natural hazard a natural event, such as a volcanic eruption or flood, that threatens or actually causes damage to people and their settlements

natural increase the growth of population resulting from births exceeding deaths

offshore moving economic activity and investment to other countries

output something that has been produced or turned out

ozone layer the part of the atmosphere, between 15 to 80km above the Earth's surface, which absorbs most of the harmful radiation from the sun

periphery an area that is lagging behind in economic development, prosperity and standard of living

plain a level and low-lying area

plate boundary the edge of a piece of the Earth's crust which 'floats' and moves over a bed of heavier, semi-molten rock

polar front the part of the atmosphere where warm tropical air meets colder air from the polar region

precipitation moisture in the atmosphere that falls to the ground as rain, snow, hail, sleet or snow

prefecture the Japanese equivalent of an English county; an important unit in the government of Japan

primary sector that part of an economy involved in farming, fishing, forestry and mining

public services water supply, sewage treatment, public transport and other services needed by settlements

reclaim to create usable land from flooded, waste or derelict areas

resource something from the environment (e.g. minerals, soils, climate) used to meet particular human needs (e.g. energy, housing, food)

restructure to reorganize companies and industries to make them more profitable

risk adjustment and reduction action taken to reduce the risk or impact of a natural hazard

risk assessment weighing up the likelihood of something happening and the possible results if it does

rural–urban migration the movement of people from villages and the countryside into towns and cities

secondary sector the part of the economy involved in manufacturing, from iron and steel production to the high-tech industry

service industry an economic activity involved with the marketing of goods and services, e.g. transport, retailing and wholesaling

solar energy energy from the sun

surface runoff water which runs off the land surface after heavy rain

tectonic plate a rigid piece of the Earth's crust which 'floats' and moves over a bed of heavier, semi-molten rock

tertiary sector that part of an economy involved in selling goods and providing services

trade friction the ill-feeling created when the trade between two countries is unbalanced; it is particularly felt by the nation with the unfavourable balance of trade

tsunami large tidal waves created by earthquake tremors; capable of causing much damage and destruction in coastal areas

typhoon a tropical revolving storm of very high winds and torrential rainfall

urbanization the process of becoming urban that affects both people and places; the concentration of people and non-agricultural activities in towns and cities

visible trade trade in goods and resources

Index

Bold type refers to terms
included in the glossary
Italic type refers to
photographs or maps